Beginner's Guide
to Successful Container Gardening

Grow Your Own Food in Small Places!

Beginner's Guide
to Successful Container Gardening

Grow Your Own Food in Small Places!

25+ Proven DIY Methods for Composting, Companion Planting, Seed Saving, Water Management and Pest Control

Written by Sophie McKay
www.SophieMcKay.com

Table of content

Quick links to the best, proven tricks & DIY methods

Before we begin, go and grab your FREE gifts!

Sophie McKay's Seed Starting & Planting Calculator
+ The Ultimate Guide to Organic Weed Management

In these free resources, you will discover:

- The perfect Seed Starting and Planting times for YOUR region or zone
- The 8 Organic Weed Removal Methods
- The 6 best and proven Weed Management Methods
- The tools you did NOT know you need for a weed-free garden
- How weeds can help your yard
- How to identify which weed is good and which is bad for a yard or garden
- The difference between Invasive and Noxious Weeds

Get your FREE copy today by visiting:

https://sophiemckay.com/free-resources/

INTRODUCTION

Growing up on my grandparents' farm, I couldn't imagine living without green spaces. Flowers bloomed in our garden all year round, and we always had fresh vegetables to eat. Living in that environment, gardening became second nature to me. Then, as a young college student, I moved to my first apartment in the heart of the city.

The one-bedroom unit on the third floor was surrounded by tall buildings, blocking most of the sunlight. I remember walking through the freshly painted rooms and feeling lost—the red maple tree outside the window painfully reminding me of home. Finding myself stuck in a concrete jungle, I longed to be out in the sun, tilling the earth, pulling weeds, and watering my plants!

I couldn't plant fruit trees and vegetable vines in my cubbyhole of an apartment. However, the place needed a touch of home to help me settle in. So, I decided to make do with what I had and bought a lemon plant. I placed it in a North-facing window in the kitchen, where it got a few hours of sun.

Imagine my dismay when—despite my meticulous care—its leaves started yellowing and dropping off. Two weeks after bringing it home from the garden center, the lemon plant was a dismal sight. After another few weeks, I had nothing but a dead plant in a container full of soil. My next few attempts with tomatoes, green chilies, and capsicum met a similar fate.

Had I lost my green thumb? Or was it impossible to grow anything in an urban setting?

My next attempt with herbs and chilies proved successful. Gradually, I learned the ropes of growing plants indoors. Moving to a bigger place with a sunny balcony allowed me to expand my urban garden and I was soon growing a wide variety of fruits, vegetables, and herbs. My approach toward container gardening became more sophisticated when I learned about permaculture. Techniques such as water harvesting, composting, companion planting, mulching, creating guilds, and building cold frames enhanced the productivity of my small garden set up, ensuring a yearlong food supply. Permaculture changed my perspective on gardening, shifting my focus from what I *couldn't* do to what I *could*. I realized the limitations of gardening only existed in my head.

Permaculture taught me that—with a few adjustments—you could grow fruits, vegetables, and herbs in homes usually considered unsuitable for outdoor gardening such as apartments and small houses with limited growing areas. Sun-loving plants such as tomatoes would thrive on a south-facing balcony, while spinach, lettuce, and mint would flourish on north-facing windows or balconies.

I conducted numerous tutorials and workshops to teach communities practical solutions for reducing food poverty. My extensive experience as a permaculturist convinced me that anyone could grow their own food. I helped my friends and acquaintances create flourishing container gardens and witnessed their joy as they ate homegrown fruits and vegetables.

My previous book, *The Permaculture Project,* briefly discussed urban gardening. I soon realized this broad topic required a book of its own. The *Beginner's Guide to Successful Container Gardening* is a comprehensive guide that will help you enjoy the perks of gardening and achieve a sustainable lifestyle, regardless of the size of your land.

In this book, you will learn the basics of container gardening. Close your eyes and picture your balcony, patio, or backyard overflowing with leafy green plants, vibrant flowers, and plump vegetables. You pluck rosemary and thyme from your windowsill and harvest fresh tomatoes and eggplants from your balcony. Imagine cooking with fresh, organic ingredients and enjoying a flavorsome meal with your family. As unbelievable as it sounds, it is possible, and this book will help you achieve it.

The book is divided into 10 chapters based on the various important aspects of container gardening. Section 1 is full of creative ideas to overcome the limitations of your lodgings and find the perfect spot for your plants. Chapter 2 will help you get started by choosing the right containers. In Chapters 3 and 4 we learn everything you need to know about soil and water management. Following our DIY techniques you can level up your skills and set up you own compost or even a rainwater saving system. In Chapter 5 we will be learning about your plant's needs and in Chapter 6, we uncover the secrets of seed growing.

Chapter 7 covers important requirements of the best fruits, vegetables, and herbs for container gardens while Chapter 8 will help you keep the momentum going by managing your plants, warding off pests, and preventing the spread of disease. If you came with us so far, we are ready to harvest! Chapter 9 teaches you all the important tips and tricks you need to know for a successful harvest. The last chapter is all about enjoying the fruits of your labor and storing your crops for later! Chapter 10 is full of my favorite food preservation recipes that will delight your taste buds while making sure not a single crop goes to waste.

The tips and tricks in this book will help you turn your home into a plant lover's paradise. It's time to do away with your doubts and stretch those green fingers!

CHAPTER 1

Gardening in Urban Spaces

The Limitations of Your Lodgings: How to Maximize Your Space

Moving into my first apartment, I didn't realize how challenging it can be to decorate a tiny living space. I think most of us face the same challenges. The furniture has to be the right size and placed in the right way to make the most of the limited area at your disposal. The experience made me realize how important it is to look for solutions that cater to *your* needs when working with small spaces. The rules for urban gardening are the same: analyze your space and find the perfect fit!

In this chapter, we will look at some of the challenges of urban gardening and discuss its numerous benefits. We will learn about the correct planning that can help us maximize our space and the different factors that affect plant growth. So, let's dive in and see what lies in store for us!

Challenges of Urban Gardening

Nothing is as rewarding as growing your own food! Delicious and flavorsome fruits and vegetables go straight from your backyard to your kitchen, so you can rest assured that your food hasn't been treated with harmful chemicals.

The entire process is in your hands, from planting seeds to harvesting.

But before you grab a shovel and start digging, it's necessary to take stock of the situation and prepare for any roadblocks that may lie ahead. Let's look at some obstacles urban gardeners need to work around.

- *Planning with limited lateral space:* The lack of space can create some hurdles, but it also gives you the opportunity to unleash your creativity!

- *Dealing with harsh sunlight exposure:* Urban gardens tend to be prone to sun scalding. Large concrete structures in the surroundings, such as buildings or sidewalks, radiate heat, which can scorch the plants. Moreover, these surfaces retain heat long after sunset, so the problem persists as night falls.

- *Adjusting the soil's nutrient content:* Lack of microorganisms and organic matter means container soil requires more attention. Nutrient content needs to be replenished regularly. Composting is an excellent, sustainable method to boost soil fertility in container gardens.

- *Facing water problems:* Soil in containers usually dries out quickly, requiring more frequent watering. Depending on the framework of your house, an overhanging structure or eave might block your plant's access to rainwater. So, you need to be extra diligent with your watering schedule.

- *Dealing with pollination issues:* The absence of beneficial insects may create problems for plant fertilization. Insects like honey bees might not make it to your plants, especially if they're on a high-up balcony or roof. But don't lose heart; there are ways of encouraging helpful insects to visit your container garden more often. I'll share multiple alternative solutions to attract pollinators to your urban garden later in this book.

- *Warding off birds and small animals:* You don't want birds pecking away at your tomatoes or a street cat knocking over the peppers you placed on the windowsill. Later in the book, we will look at ways to protect your container garden from uninvited guests.

Benefits of Urban Gardening

Nothing compares to the joy of tending to your garden and spending time with nature. The advantages of urban gardening far outweigh the disadvantages. In choosing to read this book, you likely already have your own reasons for wanting a productive container garden. The benefits are many:

- *Ensures easier access to plants:* Who wouldn't trade an hour-long trip to the grocery store for a few steps to their backyard? Having your garden in your home makes it easier to access your plants so that you can nip problems in the bud.

- *Reduces the number of weeds and pests:* Growing plants in containers decreases weeds and prevents common garden pest problems, making gardening a breeze!

- *Helps improve mental health:* Spending time with nature reduces stress and increases wellbeing. The feel of the soft soil in your hands, the vibrant colors of the plants, the earthy smell, and the joy of watching the tiny young stems unfurl improves mood, boosts self-esteem, and increases attention span.

- *Provides access to healthier food:* Organic, homegrown food is vastly superior to store-bought options. One key reason is the exclusion of chemical pesticides, which can be potentially toxic for humans if their residue remains on the food. Moreover, fresh garden produce is packed with nutrients and contains zero preservatives.

- *Helps teach children about gardening:* It's a fun activity you can do with your entire family. You can teach your children about growing plants and instill a deep love for nature.

- *Helps you save money:* It can significantly reduce your food and fuel costs. With food growing in your backyard, patio, or rooftop, you can cross running to the grocery store off your to-do list!

Analyzing Your Space: Sun, Wind, and Shade

The first tools you need to set up your container garden are keen observation and a great imagination! Decide the spot where you want to create your urban garden and observe it for the next few days. Here are some questions you need to ask yourself:

- How much sunlight or shade does the area receive throughout the day?

- Does it receive morning or evening sun?

- Are the surrounding walls dark or light in color?

Answering these questions will help you decide which plants to choose and how to arrange them. Generally, in the Northern Hemisphere, a south-facing balcony or patio remains sun-drenched throughout the day. However, this means that south-facing walls can get extremely hot. While this might make it an ideal spot for growing vegetables, you'll have to follow a rigid watering schedule to ensure the soil doesn't dry out too quickly. Usually, peppers and citrus plants thrive in this location.

A west-facing area mostly gets afternoon and evening sunlight, so west-facing walls don't absorb as much heat. Plants growing in a west-facing space get a moderate amount of sun, making many gardeners consider it the ideal spot.

East-facing places get plenty of morning sun; however, they experience extreme temperature fluctuations and strong winds. The walls can serve as wind barriers in such cases, protecting delicate plant vines such as peas from damage. Lastly, areas facing north get little-to-no sun, making them perfect for shade-loving plants.

Surrounding buildings and trees can also change the sunlight a particular area receives. For instance, a tall building in front of a south-facing balcony will end up blocking most of the light. Taking note of tall structures next to your house can help you find the best place for your plants.

Time	Zones			
	Front balcony	Patio	Kitchen windowsill	West wall
9 AM	Sun	Shade	Partial, often windy	Shade
11 AM	Sun	Shade	Partial	Shade
2 PM	Partial	Sun	Partial	Sun
6 PM	Shade	Sun	Sun	Sun

In your notes, mark with "Sun" the areas with more than 6 hours of direct sunlight. "Partial Sun" or "Partial Shade" means the site gets 3-6 hours of sun. "Shade" means an area with less than 3 hours of direct sunlight per day. Remember to make notes on the wind and extremities, like "too hot" or "frost risk".

Planning to Maximize Your Space

When planning a container garden, most people only think about horizontal space. However, you can make room for more plants by utilizing vertical spaces and including the edges in your garden design. Walls or fences are great for setting up trellises for climbing plants such as peas, beans, and berry canes, including raspberries and blackberries. South-facing brick walls are excellent for growing peach trees due to their heat storage capacity. Similarly, a south- or west-facing wall can protect citrus trees from gusty winds and provide warmth.

Another idea for maximizing space is placing the pots on shelving units or step ladders. You can also attach pots or troughs to the railing of your balcony. If it is sturdy enough, you can fasten a trough on top and another at the bottom. Hanging baskets and window boxes are other ways to squeeze in more plants into your urban garden (don't forget to secure them firmly).

Furthermore, depending on their height, you can often grow more than one plant in a pot. For example, rocket plants may thrive around a tall rosemary bush, lettuce at the base of your peas, and microgreens under tomatoes. However, keep in mind that this can increase the soil's watering and nutrition requirements.

Figure 1.1: Maximizing space by using vertical areas.

Succession sowing is another easy technique to maximize your space. It involves sowing different plant seeds at intervals of a few weeks. For example, you might grow microgreens in spring and use the same pot for your summer vegetables. While your tomato seedlings are sprouting indoors, you can use their container outside for growing lettuce. Zucchinis can be planted in containers that have been used for peas in the spring.

Principles of Permaculture in Urban Spaces

Permaculture techniques pave the way for successful urban gardening. My first book, *The Permaculture Project*, listed the 12 principles of permaculture. Since my previous book focused on small family farms and backyard gardens, I've tailored these principles to match an urban garden.

Your container garden is a little ecosystem that benefits from following nature's rules. Keeping these twelve points in mind will help you make the best decisions. So, let's look at the 12 principles of permaculture and how we can use them to design our garden layout.

Principle 1: Observe and Learn

Observing your surroundings allows you to make the best decisions. Watch the spots where you intend to place your plants, noting differences in sunlight, wind, and other factors throughout the day.

Principle 2: Utilize Your Resources

Make the most of what you have. If you have a north-facing home in the northern hemisphere (do the opposite if you live in the southern hemisphere), choose plants that thrive in low light. If it's bright and sunny on your south-facing balcony all day, pick heat-resistant plants that flourish in the sunlight. You can also store rainwater, recycle grey water (waste water from sinks, showers, baths, washing machines or dishwashers), and turn your kitchen waste into compost.

Principle 3: Make Sure to Connect the Dots

Your container garden represents an ecosystem; the more connected it is to other ecosystems, the more it'll flourish. Better connected ecosystems boast greater diversity and tend to be healthier. For example, you might encourage local insect populations in your garden to boosts plant health and reproduction, and create guilds by pairing plants that support, nourish, and protect each other.

Principle 4: Learn from Your Mistakes and Start Over

You probably won't get it right the first time around. Learning from your mistakes will help you create a better setup. Keep yourself open to change, and don't be afraid of running into problems.

Principle 5: Go Green!

Permaculture is rooted in the concept of relying on nature to fulfill our needs. Turning to green energy can help reduce your electricity bills and minimize your environmental impact. Storing rainwater, harvesting sunlight, and composting are some techniques you can adopt to achieve self-reliance.

Principle 6: Reuse, Recycle, and Repeat!

What if I told you that your kitchen bin is a treasure trove of nutrients for your plants? So, why not use it to nourish your urban garden? In this book, I will show you how you can turn waste into a rich source of nutrition and water for your little green friends.

Principle 7: Learn About Your Local Climate

Is your house south-facing or north-facing? Is it located on the top of a hill or a slope? What's the weather like in your city? Do you know the frost dates? Familiarizing yourself with different environmental factors is paramount for setting up a small-scale garden.

Principle 8: Zoom Out

Instead of fixating on one aspect, try to broaden your perspective. For example, a particular spot on the patio might seem perfect for growing your salad greens, but the concrete wall next to it might end up cooking your plant. Similarly, a heavy dose of chemical pesticides might get rid of pests like scales and aphids, but may drive away beneficial insects such as bees, butterflies, and ladybugs.

Principle 9: Look for Natural Solutions

Don't get caught up finding complicated solutions that cost you an arm and a leg! Remember, nature is your teacher. The key to all your problems lies right before you in the form of natural systems. For instance, something as simple as placing a pot of daisies or umbels next to your fruit and vegetable plants helps attract bees and other pollinating insects, so you enjoy a bountiful harvest!

Principle 10: Aim for Greater Diversity

Growing nothing but your favorite foods might seem tempting—however, the more diverse your plant collection, the greater the benefits. So, embrace diversity to create a more robust garden ecosystem.

Principle 11: Design in Multiple Dimensions

Think outside of the box. The floor is not the only place where your garden can grow. You can attach pots or troughs to the railings on your balcony or fix them on the walls to utilize every inch of space. Similarly, hanging baskets can be fastened to the railings, walls, or ceiling. Some plants that grow well in hanging baskets include strawberries, thyme, marigolds, and microgreens.

Principle 12: Learn, Grow and Adapt!

A positive mindset and problem-solving are at the core of permaculture. Nothing is set in stone. Experiment by changing the position of your plants or altering other factors to find optimal conditions. Use setbacks and obstacles to fine-tune your garden setup. Keep learning and growing along with your plants!

Temperature Zones

You'll often hear gardening enthusiasts use the term "hardiness" when choosing the right plants for a particular area. Hardiness refers to a plant's cold tolerance, while hardiness zones describe the climate of an area based on the lowest winter temperature recorded there (urban areas are usually warmer than the countryside, so take this in consideration). The U.S. and Europe are divided into 13 climatic zones according to the U.S. Department of Agriculture Plant Hardiness Zone Map. Zone 1 is where the mercury drops to -50°F (-45°C), while temperatures in zone 13 hardly ever dip below 65°F (18°C).

While usually the urban areas are a bit more protected and a few degrees warmer in wintertime, the scorching summer sun can be just as damaging for plants as the freezing winter. The Heat Zone Map categorizes places based on the number of days the mercury rises to 86°F (30°C). Zone 1 includes areas where the temperature climbs to 86°F (30°C) one day a year or less, while zone 12 marks places where the temperature hovers around 86°F (30°C) or higher for more than 210 days.

When you head over to the gardening center, you might notice plant hardiness and heat tolerance labeled on the tags. For example, a daffodil may be labeled 3-8, 6-1, which means it'll flourish in hardiness zones 3 to 8 and heat zones 6 to 1.

The Weather Issue

A plant's native habitat holds valuable clues about how to make it flourish. Plants found in the tropics usually don't tolerate extreme temperature swings, since temperature rarely varies in their natural habitat. Plants native to colder climates cope well with fluctuating temperatures through strategies such as leaf dropping (to prevent loss of moisture) and modifying their cell wall structure (to avoid freezing).

In contrast, waxy or hairy leaf surfaces such as those found on cycads and lavender or succulent stems and leaves found in cacti and aloes help plants survive sweltering heat and long dry spells. Plants rely on environmental signals to prepare for the changing seasons. Shorter days and cooler nights herald the approaching winter, activating physiological changes necessary for survival: moisture is pulled down to the roots, leaves fall, and growth slows.

During spring, as the days stretch and the temperature rises, plants stir awake from a period of dormancy and resume active growth. These subtle physiological changes are potentially life-saving, but they take time. This is why a sudden, sharp decrease in temperature during the night can cause significant damage.

Plants that can easily withstand 10°F (-12°C) during winter could succumb to a 20°F (-6°C) night in early December because they didn't get the chance to adapt. Similarly, unusually warm days during spring can bring plants out of dormancy, leaving them at risk of damage from late spring snow. You can find more info about your zone and about ideal planting times by downloading the free resources offered on my website: www.sophiemckay.com

Protecting tender crops from cold snaps or frost allows you to grow a wide variety of plants in cooler climates. With the right techniques, you can sow hardy plants during early spring, which may give you a quicker harvest. Here are some ways you can protect cold-sensitive plants when it gets chilly:

1. Move small pots indoors or place them inside cold frames.
2. Protect the base of the container from extreme cold by wrapping it with bubble wrap, a textile bag, or sack.
3. Cover larger plants with horticultural fleece or glass cloches.
4. Water plants sparingly.

Hardy Plants That Don't Need Protection

Plant varieties that are not cold-sensitive include rocket, sorrel, and lettuce. I was helping a friend of mine with urban gardening in southern England, and we were amazed to see bronze arrowhead lettuce and rocket continue to grow even when it was snowing! Other plants that can endure the winter include Russian kale, rosemary, thyme, sage, oregano, chives, parsley, and chard. However, chard leaves tend to get a little tough during the winter.

While planting hardy varieties may cut your work in half, a cold frame can significantly boost growth. For instance, lettuce and rocket show better growth in cold frames. One piece of advice that I frequently give first-time gardeners is to experiment. Try leaving some of your parsley seedlings outside and some in a cold frame. Wait and see which ones perform best.

Another point to remember during the winter is to water your plants. While frequent watering won't be necessary, forgetting it entirely will dry them out and kill them. If your space has access to rainwater, then you don't need to worry too much.

Key Takeaways

The benefits of urban gardening overshadow its few drawbacks. Observing wind, sun, and shade patterns allow you to assess your strengths and weaknesses and plan accordingly. You can maximize your space by utilizing vertical spaces and looking for creative solutions.

Identifying which hardiness zone your area falls in and buying or swapping suitable plants increases your chances of success. Moreover, protecting cold-sensitive plants promotes growth, ensuring harvests even during winter.

Being aware of the limitations of your space, local conditions, climate, and the constraints of your growing space helps you make better decisions. One such decision is choosing the right containers for your plants. The container you pick for your plant will be its home, making it one of the most important decisions you'll make. Luckily, the next chapter has you covered.

CHAPTER 2

Choosing the Correct Containers

You'll see a vast assortment of containers at your local gardening center, making the selection all the more nerve-wracking. Terracotta, plastic, resin, wood, pottery, and fabric—the options are endless! Each variety offers its own benefits. Breathable fabric containers allow quick drainage, making them an excellent choice if you're worried about overwatering. On the other hand, plastic containers hold on to moisture longer, making them perfect for dry climates.

Ultimately, choosing the right container comes down to personal preferences and your plant's needs. Let's look at different plant pots and what they have to offer.

Types of Containers

Plant containers not only fulfill your plant's requirements, they can also add a splash of color and style to your small-scale garden. There are various containers available in the market made from different materials. Each type of container has its own unique characteristics making it suitable for different plants with varying needs.

Terracotta

- They range from cheap to expensive based on their size and design.
- They are porous, drawing moisture from the soil and drying it out.
- Their weight makes them great for anchoring tall or top-heavy plants and resisting strong winds.
- They can break if they topple over due to a top-heavy plant or while moving.
- They are heavy, making it difficult to move them.
- They must be wrapped with bubble wrap to avoid frost damage during winter.

Glazed Clay

- They cost more than unglazed clay pots, but are still quite affordable.
- They come in a wide variety of colors.
- They retain moisture well.
- They can cause waterlogging.

Plastic

- They are the least expensive option for plant containers in the market.
- They are lightweight, making them easier to move.
- They are durable, inexpensive, and available in a range of colors.
- They hold moisture well, requiring less frequent watering, so they are beneficial for plants that like 'wet feet'.
- They can cause the soil to become waterlogged due to overwatering.

Metal

- They range from cheap to expensive based on their size and design.
- They are long-lasting and retain moisture well.

- They tend to heat up quickly so they are great for heat-loving plants like peppers which can struggle to grow in cooler climates.
- They are great for tender crops; however, heat-sensitive plants such as lettuces must be wrapped with cloth.

Wood

- They tend to be expensive, but can also be made from scraps.
- They can bring a rustic appeal to your garden.
- They must be lined and pierced to provide good drainage.
- They are not very durable, and the wood can rot but you can extend their lifetime by adding inner protection such as compost bags.

Fiber

- They are affordable.
- They are highly porous and breathable.
- They are great for promoting healthy root growth.
- They are made from pressed paper, coconut coir, and other grain husks.
- Many fiber containers can be added to your compost or used as a mulch layer in your pots to limit water evaporation.
- They degrade naturally, leaving a minimal environmental impact.

Sustainable Container Options

The options above come in a wide range of colors and styles so that you can customize your space according to your aesthetic. However, traditional plant containers can cost you a fortune. In the case of plastic pots, they can also have a disastrous effect on the environment, as they end up in landfills.

With a little imagination, you can cut costs and reduce environmental damage. Here are some ideas for turning household items or waste into beautiful planters:

- **Old buckets:** All you need to do is drill a few holes at the bottom for drainage, fill them with soil, and voila! You have a brand-new planter for your garden!
- **Big plastic pots:** Check with your local restaurants if they're willing to give away the giant tubs used for mayonnaise or cooking oil drums. However, make sure to wash them well before filling them up with soil!
- **Florist's buckets:** Grab some from your local flower shop.
- **Flat tires**: You can cut these in half, drill holes at the bottom for drainage, and use them as hanging pots.
- **Old sinks or bathtubs:** They might sound gross, but they make fantastic ceramic containers for plants. Plus, you won't pay much attention to them once they're overflowing with luscious green leaves and freshly scented flowers. However, this option can take up a lot of room, so only go for it if you have the space.
- **Cracked trash cans**: They're good to go as long as they can hold the soil.
- **Old boots:** Got a pair of tattered Doc Martens or rain boots? Pack them with soil, make holes in the sole for drainage, and you have a hanging basket.

Not a big fan of upcycling trash for your urban garden? Here are some more inexpensive container options that are gentle on the environment and won't stick out like a sore thumb in your idyllic garden:

1. **Grow Bags and Grow Crates**

   Grow bags are made of plastic or breathable fabric that prevents plants from becoming root bound. They are lightweight and great value for money. (They're basically just compost bags than you plant directly into.) Potatoes and tomatoes grow particularly well in fabric planters. Other plants that respond well to these pots include herbs, lettuce, blueberries, eggplant, and tomatillos.

   Fabric planters offer a wide range of sizes, some of which are as big as raised beds. They're an excellent option for small growing areas with little or no storage space. You simply wash, fold, and put them away after harvest.

You also can easily create DIY wooden grow crates, using wooden planks. Just make a frame and increase the height of the walls as your plants grow. Don't forget to poke a few holes to the bottom for drainage!

DIY grow crate with adjustable wall height

Figure 2.1: DIY grow crates.

2. Grocery Bags

Herbs and vegetables flourish in reusable grocery bags. Choose soft-sided bags with smooth plastic on the outside and fabric or flannel on the inside. Herbs, lettuce, potatoes, peas, and tomatoes grow well in these planters. The plastic used in some bags releases chemicals as it disintegrates, so only use good-quality grocery bags made with natural fibers such as cotton or bamboo instead of nylon or polyester.

3. Straw Bales

They are inexpensive and easy to set up. Growing plants in straw bales allow you to create a garden almost anywhere. Keep adding water and fertilizer to bales for ten days until they begin composting, then plant seeds or transport your plants to them. The best part about using straw bales is that there's no digging involved. Moreover, the bales disintegrate as the season ends, giving your garden a more natural look.

4. Bamboo or Jute Baskets

Large baskets make excellent containers for growing salad greens and herbs. You can find large jute or bamboo baskets at second-hand stores or yard sales for a song. You can line them either with moss or lightweight fabric to help retain water. Make sure to make holes at the bottom for drainage.

5. Hanging Baskets

Lettuce, herbs, strawberries, trailing tomatoes and salad greens love hanging baskets. However, these containers can dry out quickly on a windy day. An effective solution to this problem is using coir baskets lined with fabric or moss and checking moisture levels throughout the day. You can also use bottle drip irrigation to provide the ideal amount of water for your plants. If you live in a hot climate, then it's best to keep the baskets in the shade during midday.

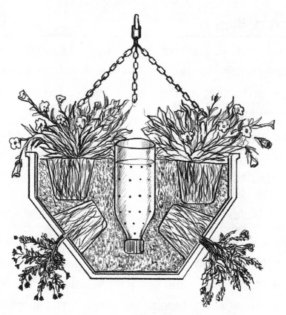

Figure 2.2: Self watering hanging basket.

Ideally, container size should depend on the plant's height and root ball. Taller, top-heavy plants require bigger containers to prevent them from toppling over. However, several factors come into play when choosing the right size of container. Generally, bigger containers are your best bet, because they're better at retaining moisture. Smaller containers are easier to move around but dry out quickly.

What Are the Standard Planter Sizes?

Pot Sizes (inches)	Pot Sizes (cm)	Pot Equivalent (U.S.Gallons) *	Suitable plants	Soil needed (cu.ft., liter) and Weight (lbs)
4" pot	10 cm	0.125 gallon	Nursery plants /Seedlings	0.01 ft3 / 0.28 l / 0.137 lbs
5-6" pot	13-15 cm	0.25 gallon	Small succulents / 1 annual	0.03 ft3 / 0.85 l / 0.27 lbs
7-8" pot	17-20 cm	1 gallon	Larger succulents / 2 annuals	0.13 ft3 / 3.7 l / 1.1 lbs
10" pot	25 cm	3 gallon	Small herbs, such as chives / up to 3 annuals	0.40 ft3 / 11.3 l / 3.3 lbs
12" pot	30 cm	5 gallon	Lettuce / spinach / strawberries	0.66 ft3 / 18.7 l / 5.5 lbs
14" pot	36 cm	7 gallon	Larger herbs such as rosemary	0.94 ft3 / 26.6 l / 7.7 lbs
16" pot	40 cm	10 gallon	Small shrubs / small fruits such as raspberry	1.33 ft3 / 37.6 l /11 lbs
18" pot	46 cm	15 gallon	Vegetables such as tomato plants / mix of annuals	2.00 ft3 / 56.6 l / 16.5 lbs
24" pot	61 cm	25 gallon	Evergreen shrubs / dwarf trees	3.34 ft3 / 94.5 l / 27.5 lbs
30" pot	76 cm	30 gallon	Larger plants: Orchard fruit trees such as apple	4.00 ft3 / 113 l / 30 lbs

*All figures are estimates and exact specifications largely depend on the manufacturer

Shallow pots that are six inches deep work well for lettuces, green leafy annual herbs, and rocket (arugula). Carrots, spinach, chard, peppers, and perennial herbs such as rosemary thrive in pots that are nine inches deep (22cm), while a depth of 11 inches (28cm) suits most other plants.

Some gardeners suggest six-inch deep (15cm) containers for many annuals; however, in my experience, the plants seem to suffer. This is particularly the case if the container is not only shallow but also small in width, which means it will hold onto less water and nutrients. As for window boxes, a depth and width of eight inches will provide enough space for root growth.

Once you've worked out the material, size, and color of your planters, it's time to decide what to grow. If you're scratching your head about what to plant, the table below will help you make up your mind.

Choosing What to Grow

Container Type	Plants
Large (18″ - 20″/45 cm - 50 cm)	Tomatoes, Vine cucumbers, Blueberries, Pole beans, String peas, Tomatillos
Medium (10″ - 18″/25cm - 45cm)	Peppers, Bush beans, Bush cucumbers, Peas, Chard, Celery, Lettuces, Spinach, Beets, Broccoli, Cabbage, Carrots, Eggplant
Small (6″ - 10″/ 15 cm- 25cm)	Arugula, Lettuces, Radishes, Spinach, Cabbage, Green onion
Hanging containers	Strawberries, Herbs, Lettuce, Spinach
Window boxes	Beets, Strawberries, Green beans, Radishes, Green onion, Celery, Herbs, Flowers

Figure 2.3: Find the right size of pots for every plant.

35

A simple way to begin gardening almost anywhere is using grow bags. Not only are they inexpensive and a great way to save space, they also help prevent overwatering by allowing excess water to easily pass through the fabric. Moreover, they are easy to store and can be reused after simply washing and drying them.

Unlike containers, grow bags are less suffocating for the plant's roots, providing them sufficient room to breathe. Another reason that I love using grow bags for my container garden is that they can be moved and repositioned with ease. Despite their numerous benefits, there are some downsides to using grow bags, which you may want to consider before choosing them for growing certain plants.

For example, they require more frequent watering than traditional pots due to fast drainage. So you may have to pair the grow bags with watering reservoirs or use ollas for plants that require high levels of hydration such as tomatoes and squash. In addition to this, large grow bags can be difficult to move once they are packed with soil. Grow bags also require more frequent applications of fertilizer to replenish lost nutrients.

Now that you know the multiple benefits and few limitations of using grow bags, let's move on to my top four tips to choosing the perfect grow bag for your plants.

1. Match Your Grow Bag with the Right Plants

Since grow bags may limit the size of the roots and the availability of water, they are not the best option for some. Generally, bushy, compact plants tend to do better in grow bags than vines. Similarly, dwarf varieties and smaller versions of full-size plants are ideal for grow bags.

Some plants that are suited to grow bags include arugula, radishes, lettuce, kale, peppers, strawberries, potatoes, carrots, eggplants, cucumbers and beets. Herbs that flourish in grow bags include cilantro, dill, oregano, parsley, thyme, rosemary, basil, sage, and calendula.

2. Use Ollas or Self-Watering Grow Bags for Moisture Loving Plants

Self-watering grow bags contain a water reservoir in the base that provides a consistent supply of moisture to the roots. Similarly, ollas are small clay pots that can be filled with water and buried in the soil to keep the plants well-hydrated. This is crucial for plants with high moisture requirements because the soil in grow bags tends to dry out faster than in containers.

3. Choose the Right Size

Grow bags come in different sizes. Extra small grow bags typically hold up to 2 gallons or 7.5 liters of soil, making them perfect for herbs such as basil, rosemary, thyme, and sage and many vegetables such as green onions, radishes, chard, arugula, lettuce and kale. Small grow backs usually hold up to 3 gallons or 11 liters of soil, making them a good choice for herbs such as parsley, cilantro, and dill as well as fruits and vegetables such as carrots, strawberries, beets, celery, and kohlrabi.

Medium grow bags have the capacity of holding 5 gallons or 19 liters of soil, which makes them ideal for growing herbs such as lemon grass, ginger, and turmeric. In addition to these, medium sized grow bags are also great for many vegetables such as okra, cucumbers, eggplants, peppers, and beans. Lastly, large grow bags can be packed with 10 gallons or 38 liters of soil and used to grow tomatoes and sweet potatoes.

Figure 2.4: Grow bags sizes with suggested plants.

4. Use the Right Soil

Remember that regular garden soil is not the best option for grow bags since it tends to be rather heavy. Confined in a grow bag, garden soil may become compressed. A mixture of vermiculite, coconut coir or peat moss, and compost keeps the soil light and airy, providing plants access to plenty of oxygen.

DIY Self-Watering Plant Pots

I remember the first plant my parents got me. I was nine years old and regularly helped out my parents and grandparents in the garden. Holding the tiny spider plant in my hand, I thought taking care of it would be a piece of cake.

I glowed with pride as the plant thrived for the first few weeks in my bedroom. I noticed the ribbon-like leaves appear somewhat limp one day and decided to cheer up my little green friend with a healthy dose of sunlight. So, I placed it on the balcony in a pool of sunshine, watered it generously so the soil wouldn't dry out, and forgot all about it.

As evening fell, my plant seemed to be doing well outdoors. I checked on it once before going to sleep, gave it another drink, and woke up the next morning to find it dead. My confidence took a nose-dive as I stared at the shriveled brown leaves. My parents examined the sorry-looking plant and gently explained that I'd been overwatering it.

If only I'd known back then how tricky it can be, even for experienced gardeners, to water plants just right, I probably wouldn't have been so hard on myself. Overwatering can lead to root rot, whereby the roots take on a soft and mushy appearance. Consequently, the plant becomes starved of oxygen, leading to its death.

Not watering enough can also prove lethal as the plant starts wilting and stops growing, leading to its eventual demise. Self-watering containers are an ingenious solution to this conundrum. You can easily create a self-watering plant pot by placing a reservoir of water underneath. A wick, with one end buried in the soil and the other dipped in water, draws water up.

Figure 2.5: Self watering container.

Alternatively, you can poke tiny holes in a plastic cup, fill it with soil and place it in the water reservoir. Place a fine wire mesh or cloth over it with a hole for the cup and pack it with soil. Water will seep into the soil in the cup through the tiny holes and travel up into your plant's soil. Keep refilling the reservoir, and you won't ever have to worry about your plant going thirsty or getting overwatered.

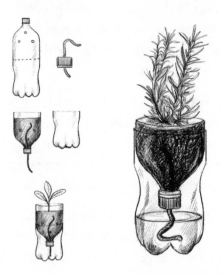

Figure 2.6: An easy DIY method for creating a self-watering pot.

Ever thought about upcycling plastic barrels for planters? You'll be surprised by how effective they are in helping you cut back on space. Empty plastic barrels can be easily turned into vertical planters for small plants. Ideally, a 55-gallon (200 liter) plastic drum barrel is a good choice. Clean the barrel thoroughly and make 5-inch (12.7 cm) slits by using a knife or drill. You will plant the seedlings in these openings. Prepare a PVC pipe by poking 0.5 - 1 inch (1- 2.5 cm) holes along its entire length. This will serve as an irrigation system, providing water to the plants.

Figure 2.7: Strawberries are thriving in barrel planters.

Don't forget to create a few drainage holes at the bottom of the barrel. Fill the planter with soil and insert a PVC pipe in the center, which will supply water to the plants. Sprinkle the seeds in the slits or transplant the seedlings. These planters are perfect for herbs, chilies, strawberries and other small plants.

41

A cold frame can help your vegetables and herbs survive harsh winter conditions. They are also traditionally used to harden off plants grown indoors or in a greenhouse in spring, before planting out into the ground or final containers. Cold frames are themselves like tiny greenhouse allowing sunlight through a transparent top, which keeps the temperature warm. This traps the heat inside, keeping your plants warm and protected. Moreover, plants enclosed in a cold frame don't need to be watered as often, as the box retains a high level of moisture.

You can either buy a commercial cold frame or build one with pieces of wood. For the base, you can use any wooden boxes you may have lying around the house, such as wine boxes. Alternatively, you can join planks to make rectangular structures. Stack these frames on top of each other until the structure matches your plant's height.

For the last frame, we need to create a slope. Cut one of the planks lengthwise to half its width—this will be attached to the front of the rectangle. Measure the width of the plank. Use the measurement to mark a spot for a cut on one end of the two planks that will make the sides. With the help of the dots, make a diagonal line and saw along this line, creating a slope. Finally, nail the planks together.

Cold frame

Figure 2.8: DIY cold frames elongate the growing season.

You can cover the frame with transparent plastic or glass. Depending on your preference, you can either balance the sheet of plastic or glass on top or attach it with hinges. The latter will give the plants more protection, especially during thunderstorms, if your cold frame lies in an area that isn't sheltered. Lastly, lining the base with plastic can help maintain moisture levels by collecting run-off.

Key Takeaways

Plant containers come in a variety of sizes, colors, and shapes, so you can customize your garden according to your taste. The container you choose for your plant can impact its health and growth. Choose plant pots based on your plant's requirements. If you're short on cash or worried about the environmental impact of your decision, recycle containers lying around your house or go for other sustainable options.

Look into self-watering containers if you struggle to get the watering just right. These ingenious pot designs are easy to construct and a life-saver for plant owners who love to travel. Building a few cold frames can help your plants brave the freezing winters while continuing to provide a modest harvest.

Good soil is the foundation of a healthy plant. In the next chapter, we will look at how to prepare the right soil. It may seem like nothing more than dirt, but it is a lifeline for your plants and provides much of the nutrients that you will eat. So, let's find out what makes it so important.

CHAPTER 3

Your Soil Decides Your Spoils

Imagine building a house with a weak foundation—it would be destined for collapse. You might not think about the soil under your feet, but it is crucial for providing plants with nutrition. It keeps them anchored and provides the necessary support to grow upright. Good quality soil is also crucial for an abundant harvest. Fertile soil has three prominent features: good structure, high nutrient content, and rich biological life.

Plant Soil Basics

So, you've got your container ready, and you're excited to start growing your own food! But, wait—what do you grow your plant in? Do you simply scoop some dirt from outside? Will that do the trick? Or do you buy a fancy bag of potting mix from the gardening center?

Container gardens are my favorite type because of the versatility they offer. They're perfect for patios, porches, balconies, and even the tiniest sunlit spaces. One of the most important factors for the success of your container garden is having a great potting medium. You'll find a wide variety of potting soils and potting mixes available in the market, but I believe the best potting soil for container gardening is one prepared with your own hands.

Hand mixing your own potting soil is not only great value for money, it also allows you to customize the soil according to your plant's needs. Also, you'll never have to wonder what's in the potting mix, because you get to handpick the ingredients.

Potting Soil Vs. Potting Mix

You may have noticed the terms "potting soil" and "potting mix" used interchangeably, but there's a big difference between the two: potting soil includes dirt while potting mix doesn't. Potting soil can be challenging to work with because it can become too compact due to too much dirt. Soil that is too dense or compact cuts out air and hinders water circulation, suffocating the roots and depriving the plant of moisture.

Potting Soil

Potting soil is suitable for indoor or outdoor gardening for growing vegetables and herbs. The formulation of potting soil offers amazing health results to plants and herbs. Peat moss, mushroom compost, and vermiculite are some elements present in potting soil that ensure maximum growth.

Potting Mix

A type of soil-less medium, potting mix boosts plant growth through a combination of nutrient-rich compounds. These include organic matter, pine bark, peat moss, vermiculite, and perlite. The large size particles in the potting mix provide excellent aeration. The lightweight texture aids root penetration. Moreover, plant growers can easily customize the potting mix to match their plant's specific requirements at various growth stages.

What Should You Choose?

The best soil for your container garden is one that offers good aeration, adequate drainage, and neutral or slightly acidic pH. Both potting soil and potting mixes offer these features, but I personally lean toward potting mix. Potting mixes are packed with organic matter such as compost, bark chips, and peat moss, which provide a surplus supply of nutrients.

Potting mixes supplemented with vermiculite or perlite should be your go-to choice because of their good water-holding capacity and good aeration. Mix without vermiculite works great for herbs, which usually don't wither if the soil goes dry. Soil-less mix is ideal for large pots that may need to be moved, because of its lighter weight. Lastly, potting mixes are sterilized, reducing the chances of disease.

The Magic Ingredients

Light, airy potting mix or potting soil that retains moisture and nutrients is the key to successful container gardening. Let's look at some materials that you can add to your homemade potting mix to improve soil fertility.

Mature Compost

Homemade compost is your best bet, but you can purchase organic compost from the gardening center as well. Mixing two parts of compost into your potting mix or potting soil can increase nutrient concentration. However, it's important to pass the compost through a sieve to remove large chunks before adding it to your mix. We will discuss how to make the best compost possible in tiny spaces later on in this chapter.

Coconut Coir (Coir Peat)

Adding one part coco-coir or coir peat boosts moisture retention and improves air circulation. It is a great, eco-friendly option made with coconut husks that need to be soaked and pulled apart before being added to the soil.

Vermiculite and Perlite

These are super-lightweight particles derived from volcanic rock. Adding one part of vermiculite or perlite can give soil excellent water-retaining properties. These natural compounds are sterile and a great addition to your plant's soil. Go for those compounds that are labeled 'grade 3', with particles ranging 3–6 mm in size.

Both vermiculite and perlite promote rapid root growth and keep new roots anchored firmly. Some of the perlite and vermiculite have chemical fertilizers like Miracle-Gro in them. Make sure to buy without these additives! You can use sand as a substitute, but always choose garden-grade sand rather than construction or play sand, since those might contain impurities like salt.

Worm Castings

You can either buy worm castings or do your own worm composting (check out Chapter 3 for setting up your own worm farm). Adding a cup of worm castings can enrich the soil with minerals such as magnesium, calcium, phosphorus, and potassium. As a result, the soil's water-holding capacity increases, making it perfect for vegetables and other plants. You can't go wrong with how many worm castings you use, since they're not damaging to plants, even in high volumes.

Next, we'll learn more about plant nutrition. We'll look at different ways to improve soil fertility and learn how to make our own soil. The next part contains practical tips and tricks for making your container garden flourish. So, let's dig in!

Nutrition Necessities

Factors that determine soil quality include biological activity, nutrients, and texture. Well-aerated and well-draining soil provides the maximum benefits to plants. Potting mix is a sterile growing medium that avoids compaction. Several additives can be used to enhance beneficial properties in the soil, such as perlite, vermiculite, coir, and compost. It's not as complicated as it sounds – I will guide you through every step!

My favorite part of the day is when I walk through my tiny garden, and let the vibrant, plump fruits and vegetables catch my eye. The delightful scent of rosemary and thyme fills the air. I glance at the bright red tomatoes and glossy eggplants and start thinking about the day's menu. The sight of juicy oranges or fresh green kale in your urban garden is sure to make your stomach rumble, but you can't expect fresh food galore without providing your plants with proper nutrition.

My favorite part about gardening is feeling the earth in my hands. I love the musky smell, the dirt under my nails, and the soft, crumbling soil in my palms. Let's look at how to prepare the best food for your plants. So, prepare yourself to get your hands dirty!

Preparing Soil for Your Container Garden

In the end, successful gardening comes down to soil preparation. Provide your plants with the right potting mix, and they will thrive. Ignore the soil, and you'll get frail, unproductive plants that are vulnerable to all kinds of diseases and pest problems.

So, what makes up the perfect potting mix? Every gardener follows his own secret recipe, like Italian grandmothers who have their own way of making tomato sauce. In the previous chapter, we established that good container soil has to be lightweight and drain well. It should hold enough organic matter to consistently provide moisture and nutrients to the plants even when the weather is dry and hot.

Generally, plant growers don't prefer ordinary garden soil for containers because it tends to be too heavy and filled with weed seeds, pests, and diseases. The process of creating your own soil is extremely gratifying. Knowing the exact contents of the soil gives you more control over satisfying your plant's unique requirements.

Usually, a good potting mix recipe contains a mix of sterile garden loam, peat moss, sand, and other additives. Let's look at some proven recipes for preparing container soil adapted from Planet Natural Research Center.

49

Classic Soil-Based Mix

Peat moss or mature compost	1 part
Garden loam or topsoil	1 part
Clean builder's sand or perlite	1 part

The organic material in the recipe above provides structure, while the sand improves drainage. You can also add a balanced, slow-release fertilizer for more benefits.

Cornell Soil-less Mix

Peat moss or coconut coir	2.7 cubic ft (75 l)
Perlite	2.7 cubic ft (75 l)
Bone meal	2 lbs (0.9 kg)
Ground limestone	1 lbs (0.45 kg)
Blood meal	1 lbs (0.45 kg)

The above soil-less mix was specifically created at Cornell University for commercial growers; however, it can be easily adapted by home gardeners.

Soil Mix for Raised Beds and Large Containers

The following recipe is for 4 ft by 8 ft (1.25 x 2.5 m) raised beds / large containers that are one foot (30 cm) deep.

Black Gold Peat Moss	5 bags (11 cubic feet or 300 l)
Teufel's Organic Compost	4 bags (4 cubic feet or 110 l)
Worm castings	4 bags (4 cubic feet or 110 l)
Organic chicken manure	3 bags (3 cubic feet or 80 l)
Therm-O-Rock Vermiculite	2 bags (4 cubic feet or 110 l)
Azomite	3 - 6 lbs (1.5 - 2.5 Kg)
Kelp meal	1 - 2 lbs (0.5 - 1 Kg)
Oyster shell flour	3 - 6 lbs (1.5 - 2.5 Kg)
All-purpose fertilizer	2 - 4 lbs (1 - 1.8 Kg)

Spread a large tarp on the ground and mix all the ingredients on it before you start filling the beds. This will prevent the formation of pockets of peat, manure, or other ingredients and keeps the mess contained. If the amounts sound too big, simply use the given proportions with smaller quantities.

A General-Purpose Potting Mix

Here's a simple recipe for a potting mix that you can use for pretty much any container:

Mature compost	2 parts
Vermiculite	1 part
Coarse builders' sand	1 part
Coconut coir	1 part

Vermiculite increases porosity, while sand ensures good drainage. Coconut coir helps boost water retention, and compost provides a sufficient amount of nutrients. You can use your own worm compost for this recipe if you like. However, keep in mind that a high quantity of compost can make the soil too dense, which can affect the plant's ability to take up nutrients.

You can add garden soil or old compost to the mix if you like by adding ⅓ new compost with ⅔ soil or ⅓ new compost to a mix of old compost, coconut coir, and sand. Adding chopped straw can make the compost lighter, if your potting mix feels too heavy.

Lastly, when preparing your mix, keep in mind that nutrition requirements vary for different plants. Herbs mostly prefer lighter soil, which can be achieved by adding more sand to the mix. Meanwhile, tomatoes grow well in regular compost.

Preparing Soil in Your Backyard

If you're working with a small patch of land, you'll still have to prepare the soil before planting. I mentioned in the previous chapter that loamy soil is best for a wide range of plants. A lucky few are blessed enough to find loamy soil on their land, making gardening all the easier for them. For those of us who aren't as fortunate, here are the steps you need to follow to improve soil quality.

Step 1: Lift the Earth

- Use a garden fork to loosen the soil. This will allow air and water to penetrate much deeper.
- Avoid turning the soil. This may create more problems later on, causing more weeds to pop up.

Step 2: Add Newspapers, Cardboard, Old Bedsheets, or Organic Textiles

- Spread these items on the ground. They will eventually break down, adding organic material which will hold moisture, blocking sunlight, and killing weeds.

Step 3: Add Manure

- Add nutrients like manure from cows, horses, chickens, or ducks. You can use fresh chicken, and rabbit manure, but cow, sheep and goat droppings are more suitable if they have aged or passed through a composting process.

Step 4: Add Mulch

- Add any organic material such as hay, grass clippings, branches from pruning other plants, or pulled-up weeds to the soil.
- Make sure to dry the weeds before adding them to the mulch, so the weeds do not root in the compost. To kill the weed seeds, you can try hot composting (maintaining a temperature of 130 to 140°F or 54 to 60°C) and rid the soil of any future weeds.

Lasagna Mulch

For big containers and raised beds, gardeners can use the lasagna mulch method. This method creates a rich layer of topsoil in a short span without the need to till the earth. The process involves adding layers of organic materials that decompose over time, creating rich, fluffy soil that helps your plants flourish. The more diverse materials you use, the richer your soil will be.

Method

1. Add a layer of manure, enriching the soil with nutrients that will lead to the rapid decomposition of the next layers.

2. Add a layer of cardboard or newspaper.

3. Spread straw or hay mixed with other mulchable materials such as leaves, fruit and vegetable scraps, coffee grounds, Tea leaves and tea bags, grass clippings, seaweed, pine needles, or manure.

4. Create an eight-inch-thick (20 cm) pile.

5. Scatter hay or straw on top as the final layer.

If you have a large container, or even a raised bed, you also can place branches, and other wood-based materials beneath the layers. Like all organic matter, wood slowly decomposes in the soil and acts as a constant source of nutrition, fertilizing the plants for several years.

You can plant immediately in your lasagna garden bed, and the soil will improve over time. To maintain soil fertility, you will have to continue adding "layers" each year.

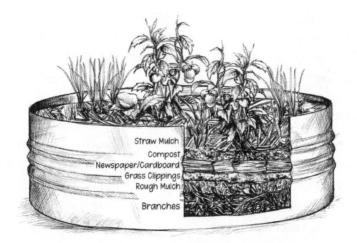

Figure 1.10: Large container with lasagna structure.

53

Composting is the decomposition of organic matter, creating a nutrient-rich fertilizer for plants. Adding compost to your potting mix gives your plants access to a wide range of nutrients that chemical fertilizers do not provide. Examples of compostable organic wastes include garden scraps and raw vegetable peelings.

In addition to improving soil vitality, composting in urban areas creates a clean environment by bringing rodent populations under control. It reduces the amount of organic waste, cutting off their food supply.

You can easily start composting with things from your kitchen bin or your backyard. Grab some leaves from your garden or food scraps from your kitchen and place them in an old bucket or garbage bin. Add a 1:2 ratio of nitrogen (fruits and vegetables or green garden waste) to carbon sources (leaves, cardboard or wood).

The mixture tends to contain sufficient moisture, but you'll still have to water it occasionally. The compost should feel like a wet sponge when squeezed (not soggy). It's important to keep checking the progress of your compost periodically. Make sure there's adequate airflow. The mixture should give off an earthy smell after a few days. A pungent, nasty smell could be a sign that something is off balance and the wrong bacteria have taken over. If this does happen, you can add shredded paper to absorb excess water, add more browns, and turn the compost to improve airflow. Ideally, the smell should go away in some time once you readjust the balance. In three months, your compost should resemble soil.

Ingredients

- *Greens:* These include food scraps like fruit and vegetable peels, coffee grounds, weeds, grass, manure, and tea bags. These items are a rich source of nitrogen.
- *Browns:* These consist of your carbon sources, including dried leaves, shredded papers, straw, peat moss, coconut coir, and

wood shavings. Carbon allows smooth airflow and prevents the stinky rotting habit of Nitrogen rich materials.

Browns & Greens
Sources for Compost

Brown Materials	Green Materials
Dried Grass	Grass Clippings
Shredded Paper	Kelp or Seaweed
100% Cotton Fabrics (small pieces)	Green Shrub Prunings
Cardboard Egg Cartons	Houseplants
Wrapping Paper	Weeds (without seed heads)
Paper Towels	Old Flower Bouquets
Straw	Human/ Animal Hair
Chipped Wood	Aquarium Water (freshwater only)
Newspaper	Tea Bags
Toilet Paper Rolls	Alfalfa Meal/Hay
Wood Ash(not coal)	Coffee Grounds/Filter
Dry, Shredded Leaves	Animal Manure (herbivores only)
Sawdust	Vegetable Trimmings
Aged Hay	Algae
Oat Hay	Green Leaves
Cardboard	

Figure 1.11: Different sources for making compost.

Materials to Avoid

You might get the impression that you can toss pretty much anything in your compost pile, but that is not the case. Avoid meat, bones, fish, poultry and cooked food, which may attract cats, dogs and vermin. Oils and cheese are not good compostable materials, while cat and dog feces may cause disease-causing organisms to thrive. Roots and rhizomes can take hold in the soil, so it's best to avoid them.

You can add some wood ashes to your pile, which can make it more alkaline if the pH seems too acidic. However, coal and cole ashes are not recommended because of high quantities of iron and sulfur, which may harm your plants. Avoid paper with colored inks, which—in some rare cases—can leach poisonous heavy metals into your compost. Also, avoid suspicious plant debris such as discolored leaves that may carry disease.

Method

1. Take a large bucket or plastic container with a tight lid or something to cover the top.
2. Drill eight to ten small holes at the bottom to ensure airflow.
3. Fill ⅛ to ¼ of the compost bin with brown ingredients. Make sure to cut everything into small pieces to accelerate decomposition.
4. Toss in the greens.
5. Stir it lightly so that the greens mix with the dirt.
6. Spray with lukewarm water. Your mixture should feel moist but not soaking wet. You can test moisture content by squeezing a handful as tightly as you can. You should be able to get 1 drop of liquid out of it but not 2.
7. Place the compost bin in an open area in a warm place, away from direct sunlight.
8. Keep checking on your compost every few days and turning over the ingredients. If you have a tight fitting lid you can even roll the bucket around to mix it. (kids would love doing this)
9. Collect your new soil in six to eight weeks when the compost changes into a dark, crumbly material with no visible resemblance to the food scraps or other compostable material you used.

Leaf mold

There's something magical about fall—the trees changing color, shedding leaves, and starting over. As a child, you might have taken delight in jumping in leaf piles, but did you know that this dead foliage could be extremely useful for your plants?

Leaf mold is a crumbly material that is created when leaves rot. Compost tends to dry out over time, losing its vitality. Before replanting in spring, you can mix your old compost with leaf mold, replenishing its moisture and nutrient content. The only downside of using the leaf mold method is that it can take up to a year to get ready. Other than that, it is fairly easy to make, involving a few simple steps:

1. Collect fallen leaves from deciduous trees and not evergreen ones.
2. Place them in a black plastic bag.
3. Spray a little water if they're dry, to trigger the rotting process.
4. Poke a few holes on the sides of the bag and tie it loosely.
5. Leave the bag for a year to turn into leaf mold.

Bear in mind that waxy leaves may take longer to rot, taking more than a year to turn into leaf mold. I personally prefer using heavy-duty bags; however, you can use regular trash bags or an opaque drum. Fall is the best time of the year to pick up leaves. Local parks and pavements are great spots for finding lots of fallen leaves. However, avoid picking leaves from roads, since they could contain pollutants.

Bokashi Composting

This method involves microbial fermentation of kitchen and soft garden waste in an airtight container. The process produces an odorless compost, while the sealed container keeps flies and insects away, making it ideal for indoor composting.

Simply add organic material to an airtight bin and layer with wheat bran that contains bokashi microorganisms. You can purchase bokashi bran online. The fermentation process will complete in about two weeks, leading to a surge of nutrients. You can add the mixture to old compost or use the liquid produced as fertilizer by squeezing the mixture and diluting it at a rate of 1:100 parts water.

The soil in your container garden will eventually run out of nutrients, making it necessary for you to fertilize it periodically. A cup of organic fertilizer mix of 5-3-4 (representing the nitrogen, phosphorus, and potassium content) and a half cup of bone meal per 10 gallons of soil provides a good start for young seedlings.

For annuals, you'll get the best result by adding ¼ cup of the same organic fertilizer during the growing season or using an all-purpose liquid fertilizer such as liquid fish emulsion. Alternatively, you can use compost tea to provide your plants with the micronutrients they need, along with fortifying beneficial microbial populations in the soil. Here's a simple recipe for making compost tea:

Compost Tea

1. Put 2 cups of well-rotted compost or worm castings in a 3-gallon (10 liter) bucket of water.
2. Stir well, allowing it to stand overnight.
3. Stir again after 12 hours, letting the particles settle.
4. Pour the mixture into containers, using the remaining sludge for another batch or adding it directly to another container.

Nettle Tea

1. Collect nettle by pulling it out by the roots or using scissors or shears to cut it.
2. Fill a bin with nettle, cutting its into smaller pieces.
3. Add water to the bucket and give it a stir.
4. Place a lid on top of the bucket, but ensure adequate airflow.
5. Allow the mixture to decompose for a month.
6. Stir whenever you observe bubbles on the surface.
7. Wait for one to two weeks for the nettle tea to be ready.
8. Strain the liquid when its ready (the mixture will stop bubbling after stirring), separating solids from the liquid.
9. Dilute the resulting black liquid and add to the soil of your plants.
10. Use within 6 months.

There's a famous gardening adage that goes something like this: "If something isn't eating your plants, your garden is not part of an ecosystem." The squiggly worms that may pop out of your plant containers, munching away dead leaves and organic matter in the soil, are called "nature's first gardeners".

Vermicomposting uses certain earthworm species to degrade organic matter, producing nutrient-rich compost. The tiny gardeners ingest organic waste, transforming it into granules called worm castings; the resulting compost is packed with soil-friendly microorganisms and has a high concentration of nutrients.

Composting aerobically (that is, in the presence of oxygen, as with traditional composting) takes time and expertise. The success of the process depends on getting the amount of moisture, temperature, nitrogen, and carbon just right, which can be challenging. In contrast, vermicomposting is easy and efficient. Moreover, the resulting soil contains a greater amount of nutrients per unit volume.

Worm Farming

Worm farming is a fantastic way to convert food waste into fertilizer. California red worms and "Red Wigglers" are ideal for worm farming because of their small size and fast reproductive rate. Here are the steps you need to follow to build a worm farm:

1. Take any old, large, opaque container.
2. Poke a few small holes (less than 1/4 inch or 0.5 cm in diameter, to make sure that the worms will not escape) at the bottom and on the sides for drainage and ventilation.
3. Place shredded newspaper or coir at the bottom.
4. Spray it with water, making it damp but not too wet.
5. Toss in some food scraps, such as coffee grounds, leaves, fruit, and vegetable peels, until the container is three-quarters full.
6. Add the worms.
7. Keep the worm bin in a warm place with the temperature hovering between 59°F and 77°F. (15 - 25°C)

8. Add kitchen scraps every few days after digging a hole in the mixture.

9. Add dry bedding if the mixture feels soggy or gives off a bad odor.

10. Check for dark color, earthy smell, and crumbly texture after three to six months.

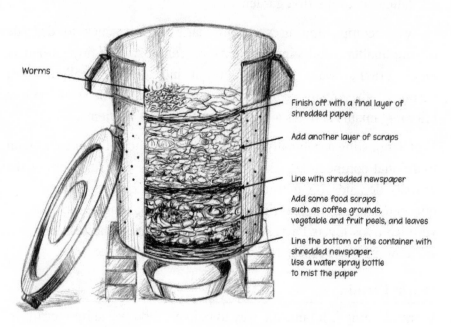

Figure 1.12: Worm Compost Bin.

How to Keep Soil Healthy

Healthy, nutrient-dense soil leads to flourishing plants, but soil fertility declines with age. You can maintain soil health by planting nitrogen fixers or mulching. Let's look at both methods in more detail.

1. Planting Nitrogen-Fixers

The roots of nitrogen-fixing plants are colonized by bacteria that extract nitrogen from the air, converting or "fixing" it into compounds that can be easily absorbed. In doing so, these plants increase the nitrogen content of the soil. You can grow nitrogen fixers in your backyard garden, containers, or raised beds alongside other plants. This technique is a type of polyculture, where more than one type of plant is grown in a single garden bed.

Common nitrogen-fixing plants include legumes such as peas and beans. You can add trellises to the north side of your backyard or balcony for growing peas or green beans. The plants will increase the nitrogen content in the soil while sheltering other plants from strong northern winds.

Most nitrogen-fixing plants, such as clovers, sprout from the soil on their own because they can thrive with minimal human intervention in the most damaged soil. However, these plants fix nitrogen for their own use. They can nonetheless be sown in autumn as a green manure and dug in during the spring. Some gardeners use clover as ground cover for their plants.

Another great way to improve soil fertility while keeping wild plant populations in check is the chop-and-drop method. It simply involves cutting nitrogen-fixing plants, prompting their root nodules to release nitrogen.

2. Mulching

The process of spreading material such as grass clippings, wood chips, compost, and straws over the soil surface is known as mulching. This helps the soil retain moisture and brings weed populations under control. Most people associate mulching with outdoor gardening, but it can also be used for potted plants.

Mulching can protect plants from rapid temperature fluctuations. Organic materials spread over the soil during fall help protect the roots and stems when the temperature plunges in the winter. In the summer, mulching protects the plants from the rising heat. Covering the soil with black or clear plastic or organic material during spring can warm the soil faster, allowing gardeners to plant crops earlier.

Here are a few tips to get the most out of this process:

1. Avoid piling mulch around the stems of plants, as this can lead to rot, especially during winter.

2. Keep the layers of the mulch thin to allow for proper air circulation.

3. Shred the materials, using them to cover the soil so that they break down quickly.

Key Takeaways

To make your plants flourish, you need soil that is bursting with nutrients. The potting mix recipes in this chapter will help you create the best soil for your container garden. The various composting techniques discussed above will help you maintain a healthy soil. Lastly, simple tricks such as growing nitrogen-fixing plants and mulching can significantly improve soil fertility.

Now that we've taken care of our plants' nutritional requirements, let's move on to another essential component of gardening: water. It serves as a medium for the uptake of minerals from the soil, making it crucial for the survival of plants. While it may seem fairly simple, it can prove to be quite complicated for beginners. The next chapter covers the plants' watering requirements. So, get ready to make a splash!

CHAPTER 4

Working Out the Water

Container gardening allows you to turn small spaces into growing areas, adding a brilliant dash of color and bringing nature to your doorstep. Satisfying your plants' watering needs may seem easy and straightforward but can be tricky to get right. Over the years, I experimented with various methods for watering potted plants and raised beds, eventually figuring out the ones that worked the best. Here are some tips to help you get a hang of your plants' watering needs.

Watering Guidelines

Plants are made up of 75 – 90% water, which makes providing adequate moisture to container gardens and raised beds crucial for their survival. Your choice of watering method can determine the fate of your garden. Here are some guidelines to help you get a good grasp of your garden's watering requirements.

1. Monitor the weather

How much water your plant needs on a given day depends on the weather conditions. Plants require more frequent watering during the blazing hot summer, while one or two times a week suffices during the freezing winter. Keep an eye on the weather and adjust the amount of water accordingly.

2. Learn about your plants' watering needs

Plants are finicky beings with different preferences. Plants native to dry, arid climates, such as succulents, like their soil dry, while tropical plants and some vegetables such as celery, spinach, and cauliflower prefer their soil moist. Look up your plant's watering requirements before deciding on a watering schedule, so you don't end up under- or overwatering.

An under watered plant may develop brown leaves with crispy, dry edges and display slow growth, wilting, leaf dropping, and leaf curling. You might notice some plants wilting in the afternoon and recovering by morning, which could indicate heat stress.

You can detect overwatering by touching the soil. Wet, soggy soil, with a greenish tinge (indicating algal blooms) shows that the plant is getting more water than it needs. Drooping branches, brown or yellow leaves, and leaf-dropping are all signs of overwatering. Slimy or foul-smelling roots could mean the onset of root rot.

3. Adopt less frequent but deep watering

The water should reach the entire root network deep in the soil to promote healthy root growth. It's better to water sparingly, making sure the entire soil gets soaked through, instead of frequent, shallow watering.

You can use a soil probe (any long metal object) to check the watering depth if you feel unsure. Simply stick the probe through the soil; if it easily penetrates the earth, then the soil is moist.

If not, then you need to water more. To avoid overwatering, make sure the top inch or two of the soil is dry before you water again. Deep watering can also help get rid of excess salts, which can cause salt burns that can give leaves brown edges.

4. Water in the morning

Mornings are the best for watering plants, because they absorb the most moisture at this time. It makes them better equipped to face the scorching sun in the afternoon while preventing waterborne diseases and pests that thrive in cool and moist conditions.

5. Water evenly and consistently

Even and consistent watering delivers the best results, while inconsistent watering can dry out or kill seeds or seedlings. Automatic watering systems are usually the best for raised beds because of their adjustable timers. They can be programmed for daily waterings during the summer and less often during rainy or cold weather.

Ollas

Ollas are small terracotta pots that you can fill with water and bury in your garden or containers. Water slowly seeps out of the porous terracotta into the surrounding earth, providing consistent moisture to the plant. They resemble a small round flask that you can refill as often as you like through the spout. Generally, you'll have to refill them more often during warm, windy, or dry weather and less frequently during humid or cool weather.

Using ollas is a great way to prevent overwatering. You simply fill the ollas to the top instead of flooding the pot and wasting water as runoff. The potting soil slowly draws water from the terracotta flask, fulfilling the plant's moisture requirements. They come in various sizes, so you can fit them in any kind of container, even hanging baskets which tend to dry out quickly. Ollas tend to be quite expensive, but you can easily make them at home by concreting up the base of a terracotta pot, burying it and covering with a saucer for a lid.

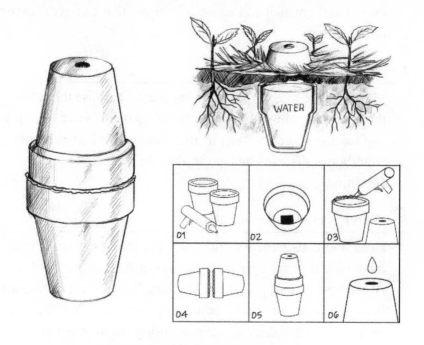

Figure 4.1: DIY olla from terracotta pot.

Roots of potted plants can't penetrate into the ground in search of water. Moreover, containers warm up faster than the earth, causing the soil to dry out. Self-watering containers can help you counter this problem to an extent. However, it's not reasonable to restrict yourself to just one type of container, especially when you're working with limited space.

Rainwater is more beneficial for plants than tap water, which might contain chlorine. If you have access to a patio or rooftop, then simply place a bucket under the gutter downspout or on the roof to collect rainwater. You can also purchase a rain barrel/water butt, which is a large container for collecting water. Attaching the water butt to the downspout allows you to collect a massive amount of rainwater.

If you're worried about it taking too much space, then narrow, spacing-saving water butts are the solution. They have a surprisingly

66

high water storage capacity while taking up minimal space. They can be attached to walls, leaving floor space available for you to place your plants. However, you'll have to buy a kit to fit into the downspout, which will help you redirect the water toward the drain when the water butt is full to prevent it from overflowing.

DIY Rain Barrel System

If you don't feel like splurging on a water butt and you have the space, you can construct a rain barrel system to stock up on precious rainwater. According to Environmental Protection Agency, a 55-gallon (200L) barrel can help you collect up to 1,300 gallons (5000L) of water every year. If that seems like a lot more water than comes off of your roof in a year, consider that 600gallons (2270L) of water lands on a 1000 square foot (92 m2) roof for every 25mm of rain. This is also why it's important to make sure you plan for your barrel to overflow even in small rain events; water should be directed away from your foundation.

Here are the steps for setting up your own rain barrel system:

Step 1: Prepare the barrels

Rinse the inside and outside of the barrels and let them dry by placing them upside down. On the top of one of the barrels, trace an opening for a downspout flex-elbow connector and cut it out (this will receive rainwater from the downspout). Cut another hole on the side of this barrel (this will remove excess water when the barrel gets full). You also can use an overflow pipe, based on the illustration below!

Step 2: Build the plumbing

Cut two PVC pipes to make a "u" shape. You'll need two 3½-inch (10 cm) pieces, two 8-inch (20 cm) pieces, a 20-inch (50 cm) piece, and a 10-inch (25 cm) piece. Attach the 3½-inch (10 cm) pieces vertically to the barrels. Connect the 8-inch and 20-inch pieces horizontally, linking the two barrels with each other. The last 10-inch piece will attach to a tap.

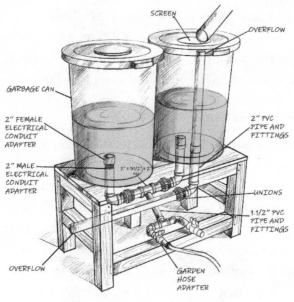

SCREEN
OVERFLOW
GARBAGE CAN
2" FEMALE ELECTRICAL CONDUIT ADAPTER
2" PVC PIPE AND FITTINGS
2" MALE ELECTRICAL CONDUIT ADAPTER
2" x 11/2" x 2" tap
UNIONS
1.1/2" PVC PIPE AND FITTINGS
OVERFLOW
GARDEN HOSE ADAPTER

Rainwater collecting barrel system

Figure 4.2: An example of a DIY rainwater collecting system.

Step 3: Create a stand for the barrels

Use outdoor-friendly wood like cedar to create a sturdy barrel stand. You'll need a frame for the top (the size depends on the barrels' size), 4- by 4-inch posts for the legs, and a border. Don't forget that the stand has to hold a lot of weight! The stand should have holes for the PVC pipes to go through. If you are connecting to a hose, it's good to know, that having the tanks higher will increase the water pressure.

Step 4: Attach the PVC pipes

Flip the barrels upside down and attach the "U" shaped PVC pipe frame from step 2. Align the pipes with the holes on the stand and glue them to the barrels. Install the overflow pipe.

Step 5: Connect the PVC pipes

Create an overflow valve using two elbows and a length of PVC pipe. Connect this to the hole you made on the first barrel. Use a flexible elbow connector to link the gutter downspout to the hole at the top of the barrel. Make the system watertight by using silicone to lock everything in place. Send the overflow water away from the foundation of the house (preferably downhill if possible).

Step 6: Fix a water hose to the tap or fill your watering can

Place a bucket or watering can under the tap or attach a water hose, and you're ready to start watering your plants!

Water Conservation Methods

Here are some other ways to conserve water while making sure your plants are well-hydrated:

1. **Water gradually and deeply:** Make sure the water penetrates a depth of at least 8 inches (20 cm). However, bear in mind that excess watering can leach nutrients from the soil. Generally, most plants require at least 1 inch (2.5 cm) of water per week.
2. **Reuse water from your household:** Collect water from dehumidifiers or air conditioners in empty buckets for watering plants. Other water-saving options include reusing bathwater or dishwashing water, provided you use biodegradable or organic washing liquid and soap.
3. **Group plants by their watering needs:** Divide plants into two groups: moisture-loving plants and drought-tolerant plants. This also helps avoid wasting water on plants that don't need or want it.
4. **Add a rain gauge:** You can keep track of rainfall using a simple rain gauge to avoid overwatering.
5. **Use drip irrigation:** This method delivers water to the root zone, minimizing water loss due to runoff and evaporation.
6. **Use water-saving containers:** Glazed terracotta containers retain moisture longer, requiring less frequent watering.

7. **Give mulching a go:** A 2-inch-deep (5 cm) mulch layer helps soil retain moisture and reduces weed sprouting.

Key Takeaways

Water is an essential plant requirement, but this important natural resource should be used wisely. The methods outlined in this chapter will help you conserve water while understanding your plants' unique hydration preferences. Simple techniques such as using ollas, water butts, and storing rainwater can go a long way.

The DIY barrel system is an excellent and fairly inexpensive method for you to save rainwater, if you live in an area that receives plenty of rain. Reusing water used for household chores and simply opting for better devices such as water timers can help you save this precious resource.

By now, we've learned methods for preparing the soil and meeting your plants' nutritional and water requirements. It's time to move on to the most exciting part of gardening: planting the seeds! Section 2 focuses on deciding which plants to grow and where, sowing seeds, and looking after the seedlings as they sprout!

CHAPTER 5

The Work Begins – Let's Plant!

Know Thy Plant

You've observed your balcony, patio, or backyard, noting the sunlight, wind, and water patterns. You have your potting mix and compost prepared and your containers ready for the next step. All of a sudden, you're stumped! What do you grow? Where do you start?

A trip to the garden center can seem overwhelming. You might feel a little lost as you find yourself surrounded by thousands of plants. Here are some tips to help you decide which plants to consider for your container garden.

Deciding What to Grow

The joy and beauty of growing your own fruits, vegetables, and flowers is unparalleled. Home gardening allows you simple pleasures like biting into a red, juicy tomato that's still warm from the sun—plucked and eaten on the spot. You can grow almost any vegetable or fruit in a container and save yourself the hassle of dashing out to the grocery store to buy produce. However, it can be disheartening to watch your plants wither and die. Choosing the right plants can help you get off to a good start.

Vegetables

When choosing vegetables to grow in pots, search for small varieties that are suited to the climate of your region (Michaels, 2022). Here are some vegetables that generally grow well in container gardens:

- **Peas:** They require tall structures to support their growth, frequent watering, and rich soil.
- **Potatoes:** Their growing season lasts 120 days, so search for varieties that mature early. Yes, even potatoes can be grown in bags and containers!
- **Tomatoes:** They require a trellis, rod, or tomato cage to keep them upright.
- **Carrots:** They grow best in deep containers. Use a pot that's twice the depth of the variety you intend to grow.
- **Radishes:** They can be grown in small containers.
- **Eggplant:** They grow best in troughs. However, bear in mind that most eggplant varieties are fairly sensitive to cold temperatures, i.e., they should not be exposed to temperatures lower than 50°F (10°C).
- **Zucchini/Squash/Cucumbers:** They require a 24-inch pot with a trellis to provide support. Alternatively, you can go for bush varieties instead of sprawling vines, which do not require support structures such as trellises.
- **Leafy greens:** They include cut and come again vegetables such as lettuce, kale, bokchoy, arugula, Swiss chard, mustard green, and spinach.
- **Peppers and chilies:** They include bell and hot peppers, which are perfect for making salsa.
- **Herbs:** They include herbs such as parsley, thyme, rosemary, and basil, which are a necessity in every kitchen.

Fruits

You might think you need a big garden to grow fruit, but you couldn't be more wrong. You can grow dwarf fruit trees in pots and enjoy homegrown fruits such as cherries, apples, and strawberries.

- **Apples:** Dwarf rootstocks of apples can be easily grown in 13 – 15 inch (35 - 50 cm) pot kept in a sunny spot.
- **Blackcurrants:** They require full sun and can be grown in a 12 – 15 inch (45 – 50 cm) wide pot.
- **Blueberries:** Placed in a sheltered, sunny spot in an 11 inch (30 cm) container, they bear plenty of fruits.
- **Cherries:** While some varieties thrive in the sun, others are more tolerant toward partial shade. Planted in a 23 inch (60 cm) container, the plant tends to flourish.
- **Figs:** A warm, sunny spot is ideal for growing figs. The plant requires a 13 – 15 inch (35 -4 cm) wide container.
- **Peaches and Nectarines:** They must be kept in a wind protected, sunny spot and planted in a 13 inch (45 cm) wide container

Flowers

Whether you're looking for a good candidate for a hanging basket, a window box, or a small pot, you'll find tons of options to choose from when it comes to flowers. Here are some of the best flowers for growing in containers:

- **Geraniums:** These vibrant flowers blossom from late spring through summer, achieving the height of 12 to 18 inches (30-38 cm). Placed on a sunny balcony, they will reward you with a bright display of color lasting all season.
- **Gladiolus:** Placed in large containers kept under the full sun, these beautiful plants range in size from 6 inches to 3 feet (15-90 cm).
- **Pansy:** These cold hardy plants reach a maximum height of 6 – 12 inches (15-30 cm), making them perfect for shallow bowls or mixed planting.
- **Dahlia:** The gorgeous decorative flowers can reach up to 2 – 4 inches (5-10 cm) tall. Some may have tiny 2 inch pom poms or large blooms as big as dinner plates at 15 inches (38 cm) wide. The tubers require full sun, can be stored for winter, and replanted next spring.

- **Fuchsia:** Commonly found in hanging baskets, they are not fond of the heat, so keep them in partial shade in a sheltered place.
- **Sweet Alyssum:** This drought tolerant annual is best known for its tiny buds and sweet fragrance, but it's also excellent at bringing pollinators such as humming birds and butterflies to your container garden. With a maximum height of 6 inches (15 cm), this small plant won't take up a lot of space. It prefers full sun, responding well to window boxes and hanging baskets.
- **Lavender:** They thrive in full sun and prefer a well-drained, neutral to alkaline soil. Terracotta pots work best for lavenders. The best time to plant these tender flowers is in spring.
- **Calendula:** They prefer well-draining, consistently moist soil. Keep in the full sun.

Now that we've discussed the ideal plants for containers, let's also take a note on some plants that usually don't respond well in containers:

- Melons
- Corn
- Large squash
- Pumpkin

Know Your Plants

In order to reproduce, plants need to produce flowers and seeds. It may seem that plants lead easy lives, but they are fast at work, trying to achieve their solitary goals. Based on their lifecycle, plants can be divided into three groups: annuals, biennials, and perennials. Knowing the difference between these plant groups gives you an idea about which plants can be rotated yearly and which will remain rooted. It will also give you an idea about when to expect harvests and seed production.

Nutritious Annuals

These are planted as seeds, sprout in the spring, and die in fall or winter. You'll have to save their seeds for the next growing season, or buy new ones. Annual plants are bright, vibrant, and colorful, attracting lots of pollinators such as butterflies and bees. Examples include broccoli, peas, beans, nasturtium, tomatoes, arugula, lettuce, basil, and cucumbers.

Some annual plants thrive in the sun, while others prefer shade. Their colorful flowers attract hordes of pollinators. They tend to be sensitive to cold, preferring warm temperatures. Based on hardiness, they can be divided into the following sub-groups:

- **Hardy Annuals:** Cold-tolerant annuals complete their life cycle in one season and can be sown directly in the soil outside. They can endure frost and survive tough winters. Broccoli, kohlrabi, leek, lettuce, onion, and spinach are some examples of hardy annual crops.
- **Half-Hardy Annuals:** These plants can tolerate mild frosts, but they're unlikely to survive protracted freezing temperatures. The seeds need to be started in a greenhouse between four to eight weeks before the last frost. Examples include cauliflower, and endive.
- **Tender Annuals:** Unable to tolerate cold, these plants require warm conditions for growth. Cucumber, eggplant, muskmelon, okra, pepper, pumpkin, and tomatoes are some examples of tender annuals.

Productive Biennials

They grow in the first year, then produce seeds and die in the second year. Some biennials may behave like annuals. Swiss chard is an example of a nutritious biennial plant that may produce seeds in its first year if it is experiencing drought-like conditions. On a ground covered with mulch, it sprouts during the spring, sending a flower stalk up in the summer, allowing gardeners to save seeds. Some gardeners prefer buying new seeds each year, considering it a much more reliable way to go. It's important to keep in mind that F1 hybrids do not replicate themselves true to form through seeds.

It's easy to confuse biennials with annuals. Carrots, parsley, parsnips, collards, cabbage, celery, beets, and fennel will bring a vast number of nutrients and vitamins to your dinner table, but don't expect these plants to produce seeds in their first season. During the first year, the seeds germinate, the plant grows but doesn't produce flowers.

It's a wondrous experience watching the plants awaken from their winter sleep and produce blooming flowers the following summer. The flower structures of biennial plants are complex and burst with seeds in their second year of life. For example, the dill weed produces seeds, dropping them on the soil. On a side note: dill seeds make an excellent substitute for caraway or cumin in recipes, making them a useful addition to your container garden.

Perennials: The Crown Jewel of Your Urban Garden

These need to be planted once and produce seeds almost every year. Examples include grapes, rhubarb, asparagus, and apple trees. Perennials give fruits and greens every season for several years after planting. They also produce seeds through flowers following successful pollination, just like annuals and biennials.

For example, even a dwarf apple tree creates hundreds of blossoms, attracting swarms of bees and other winged pollinators. How many of these flowers turn into fruits is up to chance. Strong winds and heavy downpours can deter pollination. Perennials are less finicky compared to biennials or annuals, requiring minimal care.

Why Should You Plant More Perennials?

These low-maintenance, long-lasting plants are your best bet for a container garden. All you need to do is keep a regular check on weeds and pruning until harvest time rolls in. Plants such as chives, rhubarb, sorrel, and ramps are the first to appear in spring, with harvest lasting until the end of the season.

Their deep root networks mean they require less watering, if planted in the earth, where they will be able to access groundwater.

This makes them particularly great for drought-prone regions. It also allows them to draw nutrients buried deep underground, bringing them closer to the surface and enriching the soil, which benefits annuals and biennials planted nearby.

Due to their deep root systems, perennials require large sized pots to grow well. In bigger pots, perennials plants overwinter successfully. Growing perennials in containers allows home growers to maintain a steady supply of food all year long partly due to how well these plants weather cold temperatures. In addition, growing in containers allows you to customize the soil according to your plant's needs, something that is more difficult to do in your backyard garden.

They continue cropping each year with little to no effort on the part of the gardener since they don't need to be grown from seeds. They are usually more pest and disease-resistant and quickly bounce back from attacks, unlike annuals or biennials, which may succumb to the most minor problems.

Here are some suggestions for perennial vegetables for your container garden:

- Herbaceous perennials such as rosemary, chives, thyme, and mint
- Strawberries
- Green salad leaves, sorrel, watercress, mitsuba, and Turkish rocket
- Chicory
- Daubenton's kale and nine-star broccoli (plant in an 18-inch-wide /45 cm container)
- Tree onions (they don't appear in the first year)
- Self-seeding vegetables such as rocket

Seed Selection

You're going through a seed catalog, and you're baffled by all the plant names popping up: cucumbers, tomato, carrot, broccoli—which ones do you choose? If you're scratching your head over what to buy, don't worry; this chapter has you covered. We can break down the process of seed selection into three simple steps.

1. Match Your Plants with Your Climate

In the previous chapters, I highlighted the importance of knowing your climate and planning your garden accordingly. The same holds true for seed selection. Your chances of success increase dramatically when you choose seeds that are suited to your local climate. For example, okra, which is naturally found in Africa, grows well in the Deep South because the region offers warm, humid conditions. You may not get the same results in bleak San Francisco weather.

Similarly, potatoes, which are native to the Andes, prefer cool weather. You'll see them thriving in coastal California all summer long. However, when planted in Georgia, their growth stops by mid-summer. While there is no harm in choosing a few plants that you may have to coddle to get results, sticking to locally-adapted varieties is much wiser.

A great way to go about the seed selection process is by finding your primary gardening window. This is the number of frost-free days that you get on average annually. Since most vegetables stop growing when temperatures hit below 32°F (0°C), it helps to know the average date of the last frost in spring and the first in fall.

Warmth-loving vegetables such as tomatoes, squashes, cucumbers, basil, corn, beans, and melons usually die during the first frost of the year. So, the ripening and harvesting of these vegetables must take place in the frost-free window. Vegetables such as lettuce, broccoli, carrots, cabbage, peas, and most root crops don't mind light frosts but wilt in the scorching summer heat. Cool-season vegetables planted in a northern, coastal, or high-elevation environment continue to thrive during the summer, which tends to be mild. In other places, it's best to grow these vegetables during spring and fall.

The "days to maturity" given on the seed packets or in seed catalog listings can help you decide which plants will flourish in your area, Generally, plants that need more than 90 days to mature, such as tomatoes, melons, and corn, don't grow well in cool areas.

2. Understand Your Growing Area

You can find the mature size of the plants listed on the seed packet and use this information to decide whether or not they will fit in your garden. Steer clear of sprawling vegetable vines if you have a small gardening space. Vegetables such as pole beans, cucumbers, melons, and winter squash require large growing areas. However, they can be grown vertically, making them suitable for fairly small spaces, especially in the case of beans. Beets, carrots, lettuce, onions, herbs, radishes, and carrots are best suited for small spaces.

It is also important to consider the amount of sunlight that your garden receives before selecting seeds. Green leafy vegetables may require no more than four hours of direct sunlight daily, but most plants require a minimum of six hours. Moreover, warmth-loving plants prefer eight or more hours of direct sunlight.

3. Create a Planting Plan

Astute gardeners have a yearly plan for the patch of land they cultivate. Since it usually takes plants six months to go from seed to harvest, there's time for repeat sowings throughout the season. Arugula, beans, peas, radishes, beets, and basil provide early harvests.

These plants are excellent for filling empty space between tomatoes, squashes, and sweet potatoes in raised beds (or even in large containers) and can be harvested when young and tender. For example, tomatoes are usually planted 2 to 4 feet (60-120 cm) apart. In the six to eight weeks that the tomato seedlings are sprouting, you can plant smaller crops in the space between them.

If you're new to gardening, stock up on seeds of low-maintenance crops such as peas, basil, beans, radishes, beets, turnips, and arugula. There's a lot that can go wrong with high-maintenance plants like tomatoes, squash, corn, broccoli, and bell peppers, so it's better to gain experience with easy-to-grow crops before moving on to fastidious varieties.

Your Own Planting Calendar

Download my seed starting and planting chart from www.sophiemckay.com to make the process of planning your garden completely hassle-free.

The charts will help you decide which plants you should grow during different seasons so you get an abundant harvest and make the most of your container garden.

Companion Planting

Imagine giving your plants little roommates! Companion planting is the ultimate solution if you're looking to maximize your gardening space. You simply group different plants into one pot either for their mutual benefit or because one plant improves the growth of the other.

Companion planting helps bring pollinators and beneficial insects to your garden while warding off pests and suppressing weeds. There can also be further benefits to particular plant groupings; for example, inclusion of nitrogen-fixing plants can improve soil fertility by increasing nutrient content, while plants that are susceptible to the scorching summer heat, such as lettuce, thrive in the shade provided by taller plants.

However, there are some plants that you should never group together. These include highly competitive varieties with similar nutrient, water, and space requirements. Plants susceptible to similar pests or diseases, such as blight, are likewise unsuitable for companion planting, because they could cause the disease to spread. Lastly, plants that hinder the growth of other plants, such as fennel, should be kept away from other plants.

There's a lot that you can consider as you choose the perfect plant roommates. Here's a chart to help you figure out the best partners for 17 common vegetables:

Plant	Good companions	Bad companions
Asparagus	Basil, Marigold, Parsley, Dill, Tomato, Nasturtium	Garlic, Potato, Onions
Beans	Potato, Marigold, Cucumbers, Squash, Summer Savory, Corn	Tomato, Pepper, Chives, Garlic, Onions
Beets	Mint, Garlic, Onions, Leeks, Scallon, Broccoli, Cauliflower, Brussels sprouts, Radish, Kale, Cabbage	Pole beans
Broccoli	Dill, Mint, Rosemary	Strawberry, Mustard, Tomato, Oregano
Cabbage	Onions, Dill, Oregano, Sage, Mint, Chamomille, Nasturtium, Clover, Beets	Strawberry, Tomato, Peppers, Eggplant
Corn	Cucumber, Beans, Melons, Parsley, Squash, Marigold, Pumpkin	Tomato
Cucumber	Radish, Lettuce, Onions, Dill, Nasturtium, Corn, Beans	Potato, Sage
Eggplant	Catnip, Spinach, Peppers, Nasturtium, Marigold, Sunflower, Bush beans, Thyme, Tarragon, Tomato, Potato	Fennel
Lettuce	Radish, Dill, Cucumber, Carrot, Strawberry	Beans, Beets, Cabbage, Parsley
Peppers	Beans, Tomato, Onions, Geranium, Petunia	Fennel
Potato	Eggplant, Beans, Cabbage, Peas, Sage, Corn, Nasturtium, Catnip, Coriander	Cucumber, Tomato, Pumpkin, Spinach, Fennel, Onions, Squash, Fennel, Raspberries
Pumpkin	Melons, Corn, Dill, Radish, Beans, Oregano	Potato
Spinach	Cauliflower, Strawberry, Radish, Eggplant	Potato
Squash	Onion, Corn, Mint, Nasturtium, Dill, Peas, Beans, Radish	Potato
Tomato	Carrot, Parsley, Basil, Marigold, Garlic, Asparagus, Collards	Corn, Cabbage, Broccoli, Brussels sprouts, Potato
Turnip	Radish, Cauliflower, Beans, Lettuce, Spinach, Broccoli, Cabbage, Peas, Tomato, Brussels sprouts, Mint	Carrot, Parsley and other root crops
Zucchini	Nasturtium, Corn, Beans	Potato

Figure 5.1: Companion plants.

The kaleidoscope of colors in your container garden is bound to attract some friendly wildlife like hummingbirds, bees, and butterflies. These beautiful, industrious visitors are not just pleasing to the eye but also responsible for carrying out an essential plant function: pollination.

The transfer of pollen (male gametes) from one plant to the other is known as pollination. The process can only take place between two plants belonging to the same species and gives rise to fertile seeds and fruits. Pollen can be carried from one plant to the other by wind, water, or insects known as pollinators.

These useful critters go from one plant to the next to feed, transferring any pollen that may have clung to their legs. Some other examples of pollinators include moths, wasps, beetles, and even those pesky little flies we're always on a quest to get rid of!

Tips and Tricks to Improve Pollination

Robust, fast-growing gardens that produce high yields require plenty of pollinators. If you're worried about the scarcity of beautiful winged insects in your rooftop or balcony garden, don't despair: there's a lot that you can do to entice these creatures to visit your humble garden.

1. **Plant for them:** Grow pollinator attracting plants. Hummingbirds adore herbs such as sage. Basil, dill, parsley, chives, and thyme are some other favorites. Flowers such as lantana, sweet alyssum, fuchsia, sunflower, canna lily, dahlia, and catmint will rope in a variety of bees and butterflies. You can use companion planting to grow some of these plants in amongst your edibles, so they don't take up too much space.

2. **Use special feeders:** Pollinators feed on the sugary nectar found in flowers. Hummingbird and butterfly feeders are made from plastic, glass, or metal and come in bright colors such as red and orange. They contain a central reservoir, storing a sugary liquid and feed ports from which the birds and insects can access it. Hanging these in your urban garden can help attract these useful pollinators. Remember to change sugar

water often in hummingbird feeders because warm sugar water ferments and can cause issues for the tiny visitors.

3. **Provide water:** Pollinators need water alongside food to keep them nourished. A catch basin that collects rain, or a small birdbath, can help bring in bees, butterflies, and birds. Some feeders provide both food and water; you can find them during spring or summer at most retailers, big box stores, garden stores, and home improvement centers. You can also find a wide selection of hummingbird and butterfly feeders online throughout the year.

Key Takeaways

We had a look at the complicated seed jargon we might be confronted with when we go out to buy seeds. We learned about the different kinds of plants that we can choose from and why planting more perennials benefits the urban gardener. We've sorted out the space issue by learning about companion planting and solved the pollination problem by discussing various methods to attract pollinators.

Now that we've done all the heavy lifting, let's discuss the process of buying and planting seeds. The next chapter discusses the best places to buy plant seeds, ideal seed characteristics, and the best method to plant them. So, get set and start growing!

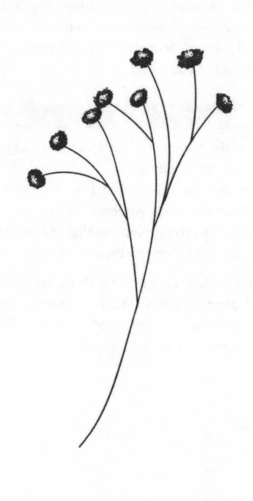

CHAPTER 6

Seed Seating

"Show me your seed and I'll show you your harvest."

—*Matshona Dhliwayo*

(Zimbabwe-born, Canada-based philosopher and entrepreneur)

The quality and yield of your harvest is affected directly by the seeds you choose. Your gardening journey begins with selecting the right seeds, which can be confusing for first-time plant growers. After all, aren't all seeds the same?

In this chapter, we will look at the different factors that affect seed quality and discuss the best practices for maximizing yield.

Where to Buy Seeds

Every year, during winter, I set off in search of the best seeds for the coming season. I order from a diverse range of sources that include various companies online. Buying from local companies is also an option that you can explore. Check out the list of companies that have taken the Safe Seed Pledge and choose the ones nearest to you. A more economical solution is to use the seeds saved from last season's produce. Sharing and exchanging seeds with your green-thumbed neighbors is also a fantastic idea to save on cash while building strong ties with your community!

Your Time Matters: Profitability and Marketability

Two factors that should play a central role in deciding seed varieties for your garden are profitability and marketability. You must think of profitability in terms of space and time. Sometimes high-yielding varieties require a lot of time and effort, making them not worth it for small-scale.

Large-scale farmers follow the same principle: regardless of how high-yielding a plant is, if it can't be sold, then there's no point growing it. For home gardeners, it's important to consider your family as your "market." The time you spend tending to your garden is valuable, so make sure to only grow those plants that your family will eat later on.

Important Seed Selection Factors

- Check the light requirements of the seed before buying them. This will give you an idea about the amount of sunlight required for their growth and whether the plant is suited to your gardening space.
- Check sowing depth to get an idea about the size of container required for the plant.
- Determine plant spacing, which can help you decide container size and whether the mature plant will fit in your gardening space.
- Consider the days to maturity (DTM), so you know when to expect your harvest.
- Find out the soil and fertilization needs of the plant. This will also help you understand the nutrition requirements and provide the correct soil.
- Determine container gardening suitability.

To give you a help on this, I included a seed vocabulary at the end of the book. Check it out right now!

You can either wait for weeks for the seeds you've planted to sprout, or you can speed up the process with a few clever tricks.

1. **Pre-germinate seeds with a damp paper towel**

    Place a wet paper towel on a tray and sprinkle the seeds on top. Cover the tray with plastic. Keep checking the towel to make sure it's damp. If it feels dry to the touch, simply spray some water. Plant the seeds in soil as soon as they begin to sprout, with the green side up. You can also use the damp paper towel technique in plastic containers or use coffee filters instead of paper towels.

2. **Pre-soak seeds 24 hours**

    Pre-soaking seeds for a day in a shallow container filled with warm water can make them germinate faster. This technique is mostly used for larger seeds with hard outer coatings. Water penetrates the seed coat, causing the embryos to plump up and sprout quickly. However, avoid soaking for longer than 24 hours, which can cause the seeds to rot. Plant the seedlings immediately in moist soil.

3. **Stratification**

    You can trick the seeds into thinking they are experiencing winter and encourage rapid germination. Fill half of a zip-top sandwich bag with moist seed-starting medium and place the seeds inside. Cover the seeds with an inch of medium and close the bag. Place the bag in the refrigerator and transfer to pots when the seeds sprout. Lettuce, carrots, celery, parsnips, and dill seeds respond well to stratification.

4. **Scarification**

    Nicking the seed's coat with a sharp object such as a knife or rubbing it against an abrasive surface such as sandpaper is known as scarification. The damaged seed coat helps water reach the embryo. Use a small pocket knife or a rat-tail file to remove a tiny piece of the seed coat. You can also line a jar with a sheet of sandpaper, place the seeds inside, close the lid, and give it a shake. Plant the seeds in the soil right after the scarification process. As with soaking, this is normally reserved for larger seeds with a thick coat.

5. Repotting Seedlings

Place the pots with the seedlings on a south- or east-facing window so they get plenty of light. If sunlight is scarce in your urban garden, then you can place them indoors under fluorescent lights for 12 to 16 hours a day. Use a water-soluble fertilizer to encourage growth.

Gradually expose the seedlings to outdoor conditions to prevent damage from the harsh weather. This process is called "hardening off" and prepares the soft, tender seedlings for the outside environment by encouraging firm growth. Cold frames are excellent for preparing tiny seedlings for frigid conditions.

On the first day, transfer the seedlings to a shady area for a few hours, protected from strong wind. Gradually, leave the seedlings outdoors for longer periods of time. After a week, the seedlings will be ready to be moved outdoors.

How to Sow Seeds

Sowing seeds may seem pretty straightforward. You may think there's nothing more to it than scattering a bunch of seeds on the soil, but there's a lot that can go wrong. If the seed does not get the conditions that it requires then it might fail to germinate. However, armed with the right knowledge, you can rest assured that your efforts will not go in vain.

Here are ten easy steps of sowing seeds that ensure success:

1. Harvest seeds

- Shake seeds from flowers or pluck them from vegetables.

- Collect seeds when the seed pods are ripe (crisp, dried out and beige-colored).
- Place them in dry paper bags (avoid plastic, which can cause mold).
- Store in a cool, dry place.

2. **Gather trays and pots**

   - Use a seed tray or drill holes into the bottom of an old cookie tin, flower pot, or empty food container.

3. **Fill containers with sterile seed compost**

   - Fill the containers with a potting mix.
   - Avoid garden soil, which can get lumpy and may contain pests or disease-causing microbes.

4. **Moisten the compost's surface**

   - Use a spray bottle to moisten the potting mix.

5. **Sprinkle seeds evenly**

   - Place the seeds in the palm of your hand and use your finger to scatter them on the potting mix.
   - Avoid covering small seeds with soil, as it can suffocate them.
   - Place large seeds one by one and sprinkle compost on top.
   - Make sure to check the sowing depth on the seed packet.

6. **Cover and place in a warm spot**

   - Cover the seed tray with plastic, glass, or plywood to prevent the seeds from drying out (if the seed packet states that the seeds require diffused sunlight for germination, ensure the cover is transparent).
   - Keep the seeds at a temperature of 64°F (18 C).

- Sow seeds in early spring (February or March) if you live in the northern hemisphere so the plants get a full growing season.
- Sow a row of seeds every week for successional sowing of plants such as courgettes (zucchini), cucumbers, runner beans, spinach, rocket, and sweetcorn.
- Sow seeds for vegetables such as cauliflower, beetroot, cabbage, broccoli, broad beans, kale and lettuce in autumn so they crop earlier the next year.
- Check the tray after a few days.

7. Uncover once seeds germinate

- Expose the seeds to sunlight once they germinate to avoid straggly growth.
- Place frost-sensitive seeds in a greenhouse or cold frame where they can receive sunlight while being protected from the cold.
- Place the seed tray on a sunny windowsill for varieties that are not cold-sensitive if you live in extremely cold climate.
- Turn the tray each day so every seed gets sunlight evenly.
- Maintain the moisture level by spraying with water when necessary.
- Keep the seedlings out of harsh, direct sunlight and extremely windy conditions.

8. Transfer seedlings to pots

- Transplant the seedlings to pots once a few true leaves (the leaves that can perform photosynthesis) appear.
- Water the compost and gently tease the seedlings out using a teaspoon, stick, or popsicle to avoid damaging the tiny roots.

- Create a small hole in the potting mix in the pot using your finger. Place the seedling inside and gently press the soil around the roots.

9. **Keep the seedlings shielded from direct sunlight**

- Keep the seedlings out of direct sunlight for a week until they form roots in the new soil.

10. **Help the seedlings harden off**

- Shield the seedlings from intense wind and sunlight.
- Expose the seedlings to outside conditions for an hour a day for a week before permanently moving them outdoors.

Seed Sowing Timeline

Like everything else, timing is crucial when it comes to gardening. In the previous chapter, I talked about the importance of planning which plants you want to grow a year in advance. By using the average frost dates in your region as a reference, you can make the most of different seasons throughout the year. Remember that a frost date is the average date of the last light freeze in spring or the first light freeze in fall. You can find out your area's frost date from the following website: https://www.almanac.com/gardening/frostdates or simply Google for your city or region by typing, for example: *"Frost date Oklahoma City"* into the Google search bar.

Here are some tips to help you plan the crops you want to grow:

- Sow seeds of cool season vegetables such as potatoes, garlic, rhubarbs, asparagus, and onions eight to ten weeks before the date of the last frost in spring.

- Transplant cold-loving vegetables into the garden four to six weeks before the average date of the last frost in spring.

- Transfer warmth-loving vegetables into the garden and start sowing the second round of seeds for cool season plants in the soil around the average date of first frost and two to four weeks afterward.

- Sow the second round of seeds for warmth-loving vegetables approximately six to eight weeks after the average date of the first frost.

- Sow seeds for cool season plants eight to ten weeks before the date of the first frost in fall.

- Sow the second round of seeds for cool season crops four to six weeks before the average date of the first frost in fall. This round can include potatoes, onions, and garlic, which can be harvested the following spring.

- Aim for a balanced mix of different vegetables every month and add some flowers in your vegetable garden to attract pollinators and other beneficial insects.

- Estimate how much you'd actually use different types of vegetables before planting. A few robust tomato plants can provide surplus harvest. You can make it more manageable by growing different varieties. For example, fast-growing cherry tomatoes can be used for snacking or making salads, big "beefsteak" types can be used for slicing, while "Roma" type tomatoes are great for canning and making sauce.

Sowing calendar

January
Outside: Nothing
Indoors: cauliflower seeds,
turnip greens, radishes,
lettuce seeds, Spinach seeds

February
Early peas
Indoors: cucumber plants,
red and white cabbage,
kohlrabi seeds, radishes
seeds, celery

March
Rocket (one early & one late sowing)
Bronze arrowhead lettuce
Parsel, Mangetout
Tomatoes, Peppers, Thyme on the
windowsill inside

April
Rocket (two sowings)
Bronze arrowhead lettuce
Parsley
Carrots (two sowings)
Basil (on windowsill inside)

May
Mizuna
Carrots (two sowings)
Plant out: tomatoes, peppers, thyme
Courgettes on the windowsill inside
Plant out basil

June
Carrots (two sowings),
Mizuna
Plant out courgettes,
Cauliflower, pointed
cabbage, Chinese cabbage,
minaret cauliflower

July
Mizuna and 2nd sow of: eets,
Radishes, carrots, chives and
carrot parsley. Green beans

August
Mizuna, rocket seeds, spinach
seeds, winter purslane seeds,
ramenas seeds,
Rocket

September
Mizuna (for overwintering under cover)
Rocket / Lettuce / Spinach
(for overwintering under cover or
outside)

October
Garlic

Prepare the garden for the
winter!

Figure 6.1: Example of a sowing for many areas in USDA zones 4-6.

93

Winter Sowing

Winter sowing is an easy way to start seeds outdoors during chilly weather. The seeds are planted in tiny greenhouses constructed from recycled plastic containers that are placed outside in the snow. The seeds germinate at their own pace, once the weather starts warming up in spring.

With no special equipment or grow lights required, this method is extremely convenient. Moreover, winter sowing gives rise to robust seedlings that don't need to be hardened off. To prepare the mini-greenhouses, poke holes at the bottom of your plastic container for drainage and in the lid for ventilation. Fill 3 or 4 inches of the container with potting soil or seed starting mix.

Sprinkle the seeds, making sure to space them out, so it's easier to separate the seedlings later on. Spray the soil with water and allow it to drain before closing the lid and moving your mini greenhouses outdoors. Keep a check on the containers to make sure the soil doesn't dry out, and the seedlings don't get overheated. Increase ventilation by making more holes in the lid or leaving it open if the temperature inside the container feels too warm.

Once the seedlings are tall enough to touch the top, remove the lids. The soil can dry out pretty quickly at this point, so keep an eye on it throughout the day and spray it with water if necessary. Winter sowing can be performed at your convenience whenever you like, but I like to wait until freezing temperatures are there to stay. It is particularly great for hardy annuals, herbs, cold-season vegetables, and perennials. If using seed packets, check the label for terms such as "self-sowing," "direct sow outside in early spring," "cold stratification," and "direct sow outside in fall."

Self-Sufficient Garden

Being a permaculture enthusiast, I'm a huge advocate for self-sufficient gardens. One of the best ways to achieve self-sufficiency in your urban garden is to save your seeds! Slice open those veggies and dry out the seeds. Place them in a sandwich bag or jar. Label the seeds and store them for next season.

Plastic egg cartons can be used as mini greenhouses for growing seeds under fluorescent lights or on windowsills. Household spray bottles can be reused for homemade pest-control solutions such as diluted liquid soap or vegetable oil. Old sheets can be used as shade cloths, while clothing items such as stockings can be used as supportive slings to aid the vertical growth of winter squash and melons. In Chapter 3, we looked at different methods for homemade compost and how kitchen waste can be used to enrich plant soil.

Furthermore, many fruits and vegetables can be preserved by turning surplus harvest into purees, pastes, and jams. Canning, freezing, pickling and dehydrating are some other methods that we can use for food storage. These techniques ensure a steady food supply all year long.

Key Takeaways

You can purchase seeds from a number of different seed companies or save your own seeds. Seed sowing is a simple and straightforward method that requires some careful attention. Gradual exposure to outdoor conditions helps tiny seedlings adjust to harsh weather. However, winter sowing does not require the seeds to be hardened off.

Seeds grown with meticulous care give rise to leafy green vegetables and delicious fruits. In the next chapter, we will take a closer look at various plants and their unique requirements. We will look at techniques and practices to keep your plants healthy and happy. Let's see what it takes to make your plants smile!

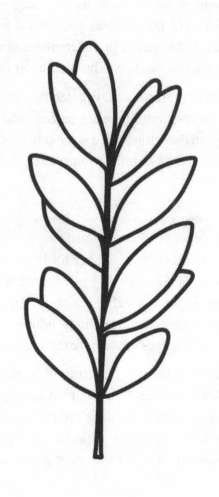

CHAPTER 7

The Plant Directory: Take Your Pick!

Fresh-off-the-vine tomatoes, crisp spinach, flaming peppers, and delightful squash—everything within your reach! No, it's not just a dream! With a little effort, you'll soon enjoy fresh produce season after season from your own container garden.

Let's look at some plants that are perfect for containers, so you get off to a good start!

Vegetables

Check the hardiness chart for your region to see which vegetables will grow best in your area. Timing plays a crucial role in choosing plants. Tender warm-season plants are your go-to choice for late spring or summer. These plants can't tolerate frost or plunging nighttime temperatures below 55°F (13°C). Meanwhile, hardy and half-hardy cool-season plants are suitable for fall vegetable gardens.

Here are some vegetables that you can grow in your urban garden for early success:

Runner Beans

- Sow indoors during mid-spring or keep the pots outdoors in late spring.
- Bury large seeds 2 inches (5 cm) into the compost and maintain a space of 6 inches (15 cm) between the seeds.
- Pick a deep container with a diameter of 18 inches (45 cm).
- Add a sturdy support, at least 6 foot (180 cm) tall.
- Place the beans in a sunny area that is protected from strong winds.
- Avoid letting the soil dry out, since these plants require high moisture levels.
- Tie young plants to the supports and apply fertilizer weekly once flowers appear. (You can easily make your own fertilizer based on Chapter 3)
- Pick young beans to encourage more crops.

Green Beans

- Press seeds 2 inches (5 cm) into the soil in small pots.
- Keep them indoors during mid-spring.
- Move transplanted seedlings outdoors from late spring to early summer.
- Protect the seeds from frost and keep under warm conditions to trigger germination.
- Use a deep container with an 18-inch (45 cm) diameter and leave a space of 8 inches (20 cm) between the plants.
- Make sure to harden off the seedlings before moving them outdoors.
- Keep the seedlings in full sun, sheltered from strong winds.
- Provide a 6 ft (180 cm) support for climbing varieties.
- Keep the soil consistently moist and fertilize when flowers appear.

Radishes

- Sow these fast-growing, low-maintenance plants from early spring until fall.
- Protect early and late sowings from cold weather.

- Place the containers in shade during the summer.
- Sow the seeds ¾ inches (2 cm) into the soil and keep the rows 6 inches (15 cm) apart.
- Keep the soil well watered.
- Prune radishes regularly to make space.
- Sow summer radishes an inch apart and winter types 4 inches (10 cm) apart.
- Pick summer radishes as soon as they mature.
- Harvest radishes when they are small and sweet and prepare fresh sowings to maintain a steady supply.

Peas

- Sow early peas outdoors during early spring or late winter if your region has moderate climate.
- Sow other varieties such as snow peas and sugar snaps from mid-spring to early summer.
- Press the seeds an inch into the soil, almost 2 inches apart.
- Use a pot with a 12-inch (30 cm) diameter and keep it in a sunny spot.
- Water regularly and fertilize weekly, especially when flowers appear.

Leafy Greens

Chard

- Sow the seeds in the final pots or grow seedlings in seed trays.
- Sow seeds ½ inches (1.5 cm) deep during late spring for summer harvest and late summer for winter and spring harvest.
- Plant the seedlings 4 inches (10 cm) apart for baby leaf varieties or 1 foot (30 cm) apart for impressive mature varieties.
- Choose a large pot and keep in full sun or light shade.

Kale

- Sow the seeds in trays indoors from mid to late spring.
- Cover the seeds with an inch (2.5 cm) of soil.

- Keep the soil moist by watering regularly until the seeds germinate.
- Harden off the seedlings before moving them outdoors.
- Transplant the seedlings to pots in early summer.
- Add liquid feed with nitrogen-rich fertilizer in early spring.
- Harvest the outer leaves in two months.

Lettuce/Rocket/Sorrel

- Sow the seeds during spring in the final pot and cover with a thin layer of soil.
- Place the seeds 4 inches (10 cm) apart.
- Water the soil and keep the pots outdoors or indoors.
- Harden off the seedlings before moving outdoors.

Roots

Carrots

- Use a hanging pot or wrap the edge of the pot with fine mesh to ward off pests such as carrot flies, slugs, and snails.
- Freeze the seeds for a few days before sowing them so they experience a bigger temperature change when sown. This will trigger faster germination.
- Sow every few weeks from early spring to late summer.
- Use quick-cropping varieties such as round-rooted and short-type carrots, which do well in pots.
- Use grow bags or pots that are at least 10 inches (25 cm) wide and deep.
- Sow seeds ½ inches (1.5 cm) deep and keep a distance of 6 inches (15 cm) between them or scatter thinly on the soil.
- Water consistently but avoid overwatering.
- Harvest 12 weeks after sowing.

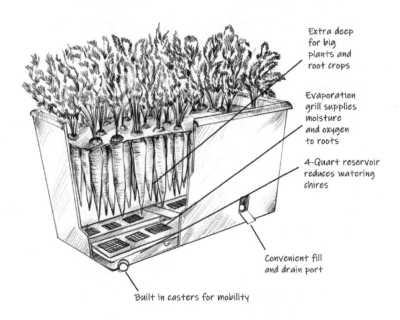

Figure 7.1: Growing carrots in plastic containers.

Beets

- Use 10-inch-deep (25 cm) containers to get good sized beets.
- Choose bolt-resistant varieties and sow in early spring.
- Sow other varieties from mid-spring to late summer.
- Sow seeds ¾ inch (2 cm) deep and space 2 inches (5 cm) apart. Repeat every few weeks to maintain a constant supply through summer and fall.
- Water consistently to prevent the soil from drying out.
- Thin the leaves two to three times when they are 3 to 4 inches (7-10 cm) tall.
- Harvest small salad beets in nine weeks and large roots in three months.
- Pull the roots gently by twisting.

Potatoes

- Use a large pot, growing bins, heavy duty plastic bags or buckets with holes drilled at the bottom.
- Allow seed potatoes to sprout in early spring by placing them in a wooden/cardboard box with ventilation.

- Place the ends with the most eyes upward and keep the egg boxes on a cool windowsill.
- Transplant to pots or grow bags when the shoots are ¾ inch (2 cm) long during mid to late spring.
- Fill a third of a growing bin or large pot with compost and evenly space five potatoes at the surface with the shoots facing up.
- Cover the potatoes with 6 inches (15 cm) of compost and water thoroughly.
- Add compost around the plants periodically as they grow, since this encourages more tubers to form, prevents crop damage due to light exposure, and minimizes frost damage.
- Water consistently.
- Harvest when the plants begin flowering.

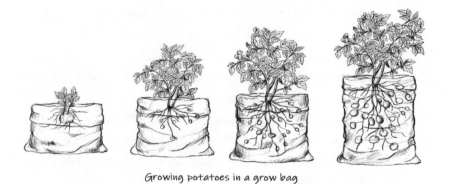

Growing potatoes in a grow bag

Figure 7.2: the bags grow with the plant.

Fruits

Chilies and Sweet Peppers

- Sow seeds indoors during early spring.
- Harden off the seedlings before moving outdoors.
- Use an 8-inch-deep (20 cm) pot for each plant and place in a sunny spot.
- Avoid overwatering peppers or feeding them excessive fertilizer.

- Mist the plants with water when they are flowering.
- Add fertilizer once every two weeks after the fruit forms.
- Tie the stems to stakes to provide support and pick fruits when green and immature to encourage growth of more crops.

Eggplants

- Sow seeds indoors during early spring on a warm windowsill.
- Transfer young plants to 8-inch (20 cm) pots and move outdoors if the nights are frost free.
- Place in a sunny, sheltered spot.
- Provide high humidity by misting with water frequently or placing the pots on trays filled with water or gravel.
- Pinch out the tips of the plants when they reach a height of 8 inches (20 cm) to make them bushier.
- Add fertilizer every two weeks and keep the soil well watered.
- Tie the stems to stakes to provide support.
- Harvest the fruits when they are shiny and plump.
- Cut the fruits with pruners or a knife instead of pulling them off.

Tomatoes

- Sow seeds indoors during early spring and transfer to pots when grown.
- Use a 10-inch-wide (25 cm) pot and fill it with compost upto 2 inches (5 cm) below the rim.
- Plant the tomatoes deep in the soil.
- Provide support for tall cordon (indeterminate) varieties by using tall bamboo canes or sturdy stakes. Bush and trailing varieties do not require support.
- Tie the stems loosely to stakes with garden twine as the plant grows.
- Pinch-out side shoots (also called suckers) growing between the main stem and leaves in cordon varieties.
- Leave side shoots in bush-type tomato plants.
- Apply fertilizer each week and add extra compost if the roots become exposed.

- Pinch out the growing tip when the plant reaches the top of its stake.

Zucchinis

- Sow indoors an inch (2.5 cm) deep in small pots during mid spring or sow outdoors during late spring.
- Harden off young plants before transferring to large pots or growing bags to avoid frost damage.
- Keep in a sunny, sheltered spot.
- Water consistently and add fertilizer every week.
- Cut the fruits with a knife or twist near the stem.

Cucumbers

- Place ridge type cucumbers in a warm, sheltered space in fertile, well-drained soil mix.
- Keep smooth-skinned, long varieties under cover and provide lots of heat.
- Choose "all-female" cultivars, since pollinated fruits generally taste bitter.
- Sow seeds an inch deep in the compost and keep indoors during mid-spring.
- Harden off ridged cucumbers before moving them outdoors to avoid frost damage.
- Cover young plants with cloches during winter.
- Train the sprawling plants up a trellis, stake, or netting.
- Water consistently and add some fertilizer once fruiting begins.
- Harvest the fruits as they mature during mid-summer to promote more crops.

Berries and Currants

Strawberries

- Use hanging baskets to protect from pests and place them in a bright, sunny area.
- Line the basket with durable plastic so the compost retains moisture and make drainage holes.

- Fill the basket with multipurpose compost mixed with water-retaining crystals.
- Keep the soil consistently moist.
- Cover fruits with nets to protect from birds.
- Apply liquid fertilizer every two weeks after the fruits appear.

Blackberries

- Choose an 18-inch pot and fill it with soil-based compost.
- Place in full sun or partial shade.
- Support the stems by using stakes or trellis.
- Use netting to protect the fruit from birds.
- Water regularly and don't let the soil dry out.
- Add a new layer of compost mixed with all-purpose granular fertilizer in spring.
- Prune dead, diseased, and damaged plant parts as well as branches that cross over one another to increase airflow. It's best to prune the bushes during March.
- Repot the plants every two years.

Blackcurrants

- Plant from late fall to late winter in deep, 18-inch-wide containers.
- Use a soil and compost mix.
- Keep in a sheltered area in full sun or partial shade.
- Add fertilizer from spring to early summer.
- Keep the plants well watered.
- Prune by cutting a quarter to a third of the branches annually, targeting unproductive, weak growth.
- Make the cuts low down to encourage strong growth near the base by removing weak shoots and dead wood.

Stems and Bulbs

Onions

- Keep them close to carrots to repel carrot flies.

- Choose a large pot with good drainage and keep it in a sunny spot outside.
- Fill the containers with multipurpose compost and press the seeds ¾ inch deep during spring.
- Space the seedlings 4 inches (10 cm) apart.
- Keep the soil consistently moist; however, avoid overwatering or over fertilization.
- Harvest the bulbs throughout summer or as required.

Rhubarb

- Plant the young plants, known as "crowns," in early winter or early spring in well-draining, 12-inch-wide (30 cm) pots.
- Use a mixture of well-rotted manure and compost.
- Add water-retaining crystals to help the soil retain moisture.
- Block sunlight by placing a bucket or terracotta pot over the plant from late winter until early spring. This will give rise to pale pink, sweet tasting stems.
- Apply all-purpose fertilizer and add a new layer of compost in early spring.
- Harvest the stems from spring till early summer by twisting and pulling at the base.
- Avoid harvesting during the first year, allowing the plants to build a strong root system first.

Garlic

- Grow from garlic cloves in a large, deep, well-draining pot placed in direct sunlight.
- Fill the pot with multipurpose compost.
- Press firm, healthy cloves an inch into the compost in fall or late winter with the pointy end facing up.
- Keep the cloves 6 inches (15 cm) apart.
- Keep the soil well watered; however, avoid overwatering.
- Harvest mature bulbs in late summer.

This might surprise you, but provided with the right care, many fruit trees flourish in pots, producing an abundant harvest. You can have apples, pears, peaches, apricots, nectarines, cherries, figs, and plums growing on your balcony and enjoy these delicious fruits all year round.

It's important to choose trees grafted on dwarf root stocks or buy compact varieties. Use containers with a 20 inch (50 cm) diameter, filled with soil and compost mix. Ensure good drainage and keep the soil moist at all times. A sunny patio or balcony where the plants are sheltered by strong winds works best. Each spring, apply an all-purpose granular fertilizer or compost, and transfer the plants to slightly bigger pots every year. A warm, south-facing wall is perfect for peaches and figs; however, the plants may require more frequent watering.

Let's look at the requirements of some common dwarf trees:

Dwarf Peach Trees

- Move the pots indoors during winter to avoid frost damage and minimize the risk of peach leaf curl.
- Encourage pollination by using a soft brush to dust the flowers.

Fig Trees

- Choose narrow pots that restrict root growth, which encourages more fruit.
- Place the pots next to a sunny wall and move indoors in winter.
- Remove green fruits that fail to ripen in late fall.

Cherries

- Train them against a wall or a fence.
- Use net pots for grown trees to save fruits from birds.
- Prune the fruiting stems after harvest.

Apricots

- Grow against a sunlit wall during summer.

- Cover the blossoms with fleece during winter.
- Remove the fleece bags on warm days to allow pollination.

Apples

- Use large pots with good drainage and place them on a sunny site.
- Protect from strong winds, allowing insects to pollinate the flowers and preventing the containers from getting knocked over.
- Choose young trees (two or three years old) that are grafted on dwarf rootstocks.
- Add a layer of gravel or broken clay pots over the drainage hole.
- Add soil-based compost mixed with a slow-release fertilizer.
- Water well and use mulch of well-rotted manure or compost, making sure to leave some space around the stem.

Lemons

- Plant in well-draining pots and line the drainage hole with gravel or broken clay pot pieces before adding the soil and compost mix.
- Place in a bright, sunlit spot or partial shade.
- Move the plants indoors during winter to protect from frost damage.
- Protect from excessive heat: 90°F (32°C) or above.
- Water when the top layer dries out; however, don't let the soil dry out completely, as this may cause leaf dropping.

Herbs

Herbs are excellent for beginners. They take up the tiniest of spaces, fitting snugly inside hanging baskets or in pots among other crops. Choose from a selection of perennials such as marjoram and thyme. These plants are adapted to hot, dry weather, requiring a well-draining soil and plenty of sunshine. Other herbs that are fairly easy to grow include mint and chives that prefer moist soil and partial shade.

Annual herbs like basil and cilantro can be sown in batches from spring onward to ensure a continuous supply. Parsley can be sown in early spring or you can buy young plants from the nursery for a year-long harvest until the next spring, when the plants begin seeding.

While herbs love well-draining soil, keep the compost consistently moist, since dry soil can cause the plants to start producing seeds rapidly. Use a generous amount of herbs in your cooking, because regular picking encourages new growth, causing the plants to become bushy. Keep the pots on a sunny windowsill indoors during fall so their growth does not slow down with the drop in temperature.

A range of undemanding herbs such as marjoram, chives, and basil thrive in hanging baskets, creating a bold display of bright green foliage. Shrubby herbs such as rosemary, sage, and bay do well in containers as decorative evergreens. Both sage and rosemary are fast-growing plants worth investing in, especially if you intend to train one into a topiary. Plant these shrubby herbs in a soil-based compost and place in full sun.

Rosemary and sage must be trimmed after flowering to keep the plants compact and encourage new growth. Similarly, snip the tips of bay shoots to maintain a tidy, bushy appearance. Regular watering is a must for all herbs; however, bay and rosemary need to be covered with fleece during winters to protect them from the cold. Repot the plants in slightly larger pots every two years to keep them flourishing.

Making an Herb Pot

A wide range of herbs can be grown together in a single pot. It's important to choose plants that prefer the same growing conditions. For example, do not add mint to a pot with other plants, since it spreads rapidly and may overwhelm its neighbors. You can repot the herbs into bigger pots after a season or two.

Here is a step-by-step guide to make your own herb pot:

1. Pick a large container with holes on the sides. You can also drill holes on the sides of a terracotta container for trailing plants.

2. Place broken clay pot pieces over the drainage hole at the bottom.
3. Fill with soil and compost mix.
4. Place creeping and trailing plants in the holes after wrapping their leafy stems with newspaper and pushing them through the holes.
5. Remove the newspaper after the planting and repeat for each hole.
6. Cover the roots with compost.
7. Water well.

Key Takeaways

Fresh vegetables, fruit trees, juicy berries, and aromatic herbs—you can grow almost anything in your urban garden. With so many diverse plants to choose from, you might worry about your gardening space being big enough to fit them all. Should you cram your balcony or patio with pots or settle for less?

We discussed companion planting briefly in Chapter 5. The next part is packed with practical tips to help you put companion planting to good use, so you don't miss out on your favorite plants because of limited space. So, let's look at some clever ways for you to squeeze more plants into your urban garden.

Practical Tips and Proven Companion Planting Recipes

Whether you have a tiny windowsill, a sunny balcony, or a spacious patio, you can fulfill your nutritional requirements by growing multiple plants in the same pots or using different sizes of containers. Grouping plants with similar requirements also makes it easier to look after them. Let's look at some planting recipes that can help you grow more plants, save space, and cut your work in half!

Herb Cocktail

Resilient herbs are perfect for first-time plant growers. They can be picked for a long season and they come in handy in the kitchen. You can grow a wide variety of herbs in a single pot; however, it's best to grow parsley separately because it tends to seed in its second year and may need to be replaced. A great combination includes pairing thyme, marjoram, chives, and sage with trailing plants such as brachyscome and petunias.

Choose large containers at least 10 inches (25 cm) in diameter or small pots about 6 inches (15 cm) in diameter. Place the pots in a sunny area close to the kitchen and fill them with classic soil-based potting mix. Here is a list of herbs that I like to plant together in my herb pot:

1. 1 x Golden marjoram
2. 1 x Parsley
3. 1 x Variegated sage
4. 1 x Bay
5. 1 x Chives
6. 1 x Golden lemon thyme

Plant the herbs in spring after the last frost in well-draining containers. I like to plant thyme and flowers in the holes in the sides of a large herb pot and place the other herbs on the top. You might also plant a small container with parsley and flowers. Keep the soil consistently moist during the summer and water less frequently when the temperature drops. Move the herbs to bigger containers every two years.

Mediterranean Delight

Think of bright-colored, sweet-smelling flowers and delicious vegetables growing in a sunny corner. This combination includes a wide range of tomato varieties, pairing striped "Tigerellas" with cherry tomatoes and "Sungolds". The addition of eggplants adds to this recipe's aesthetic appeal, as do fiery orange marigolds.

Choose pots with a 10-inch diameter for tomatoes and eggplants and 6-inch (15 cm) diameter for marigolds. A sun-baked balcony or patio where the plants will be protected from strong winds is perfect for the exuberant display of a Mediterranean mix.

Let's look at the plants that go into this exotic combination:

1. A pot of marigold (Calendula)
2. 1 x Eggplant
3. 1 x Sungold tomato
4. 1 x Tigerella tomato
5. 1 x Cherry tomato

Make sure to harden off young tomatoes and eggplants in late spring, and ensure adequate drainage. Add stakes to support tomatoes and water consistently, making sure the soil doesn't dry out. Apply tomato fertilizer once a week after the first fruits appear.

Salads Galore

The colorful salad leaves, edible flowers, and herbs in this recipe will be ready for picking in just six weeks. All you need is a large metal bucket for growing purple and green lettuces and a wicker basket for "Black Seeded Simpson" lettuce and mustard with a dash of edible marigolds. Variegated lemon thyme in the third pot adds a splash of color and fragrance while the feathery cosmos produce daisy-like flowers in the summer. You can pick the leaves individually from across the display and the plants will keep cropping for weeks. An 8 x 8-inch (20 x 20 cm) metal tub or container placed under full sun or partial shade works perfectly for this set up. Of course, you can also go for other types of containers - these are only my favorite examples for both function and beauty.

You'll need the following plants for this recipe:

1. A packet of lettuce "Dazzle" seeds
2. A packet of "Green Frills" seeds
3. A packet of lettuce "Black Seeded Simpson" seeds
4. 2 pots of marigolds (Calendula)
5. A packet of mustard "Red Giant" seeds
6. 1 x Lemon thyme
7. 3 x Cosmos (optional)

Line the basket with durable plastic and poke a few holes to ensure good drainage. Fill with compost and plant thyme and marigolds during mid-spring. Wait for the weather to warm up before planting cosmos. For Black Seeded Simpson lettuce, level the soil and sow thinly along with mustard seeds. Mark diagonal bands in the tub and thinly sow purple and green lettuce so they do not mix. Cover with a light layer of compost and water generously.

Chilies and Peppers

Spice up your urban garden by adding a colorful collection of chili peppers and sweet peppers. These small, bushy plants produce white flowers followed by fruits that ripen to brilliant shades of orange, red, yellow, and purple. The jewel-colored fruits can be complemented by zesty golden marjoram and trailing Mexican daisies (*Erigeron karvinskianus*), since they all thrive in well-draining soil and bright sunlight.

The pots for this set up should have an 8-inch diameter. Sheltered patios or balconies that receive plenty of sunshine work best for the combination of plants in this recipe.

Here are the plants you'll need:

1. 1 x Chili pepper "Numex Twilight"
2. 1 x Chili pepper "Fresno"
3. 1 x Sweet pepper "Sweet Banana"
4. 1 x *Erigeron karvinskianus*
5. 1 x Golden marjoram

Harden off the peppers and chili plants before moving them outside after the frosts end. Cover the drainage holes with a layer of broken clay pot pieces before adding compost. Water the soil when the surface feels dry to the touch and add fertilizer every two weeks after fruits appear. Use stakes to support the fruit-laden plants from drooping.

Barbecue Heaven

Imagine having a barbecue on your patio and having all the vegetables that you'll need close by. The containers in this recipe are bursting with vegetables that go straight to the grill. Think zucchini with its huge leaves and golden flowers, edible nasturtium flowers perfect for salads, and freshly picked corn cobs that taste divine when roasted over coals. Finish the display with a pot of sweet pepper plant and your barbeque mix is ready to go!

Containers should be 32 inches (80cm) in diameter and filled with soil-based compost mixed with well-rotted manure. A sunny sheltered patio is the perfect spot for this set up.

1. 1 x Zucchini "Safari"
2. 4 x nasturtium (Tropaeolum) "Red Wonder"
3. 3 x "Earlybird" corns
4. 1 x pepper "Redskin"

Wait until after the last frost before planting zucchini, peppers, and corn outside. Plant corn at the back in the pots and zucchini at the front with nasturtiums in between. The peppers go in another smaller pot. Water regularly to prevent the soil from drying out. Add fertilizer every two weeks from when the plants produce their first fruits.

Root Veggie Mix

A shabby chic collection of rustic wooden crates, chipped terracotta pots, and an old burlap bag make the perfect combination for beets, carrots, and potatoes. A sprinkle of cosmos adds a dash of tiny magenta flowers completing the eye-catching display.

Wooden crates should be 20 inches x 8 inch (50 x 20 cm) in size while terracotta pots should be 6 inches (15 cm) in diameter. The two containers paired with a large burlap bag are all you need for your veggie mix. Fill the bag and the containers with soil and compost mix and place in a sunny spot where the plants are shielded from strong winds.

Here are the plants that you'll need:

1. 3 x Cosmos bipinnatus "Sonata" plants
2. A packet of beet "Boltardy" seeds
3. A packet of carrot "Resistafly"
4. 3 x seed potatoes, e.g., 'Kestrel'

Make sure to pre-germinate the seed potatoes in early spring (Refer to Chapter 6: *Giving Your Seeds a Head Start*) and line the crates with plastic. Use a fork to pierce tiny holes in the plastic lining for drainage. Thinly sow carrot and beet seeds in mid-spring and cover with a light layer of compost. Fill one-third of the burlap bag with compost for the potatoes. Almost 6 inches (15 cm) of compost should be layered on top of the seed potatoes. Keep adding compost as the potatoes grow and plant the cosmos in the pot with the weather warms up. Maintain consistent watering and add a balanced liquid fertilizer every two weeks.

Seasonal Crop Planner

Mixing and matching plants with similar growing requirements makes it easier to care for your garden. Check out the sunlight, moisture, and nutritional needs of your plants and try to come up with some recipes of your own. Have a look at the seasonal crop planner, so you can get an idea about which plants you can grow together in different weather. The planner will also help you allocate tasks to different seasons, so you have your work cut out for you for an entire year.

Early Spring	Outdoors	Shade
Sow	corn salad, fennel, kale, kohlrabi, leeks, lettuce, onions, parsley, peas, arugula, beets, carrots, chives, chop suey greens, cilantro, radishes, scallions, spinach, Swiss chard, tarragon	carrots, celery root, corn, cucumbers, dwarf French beans, eggplants, lettuce, microgreens, alpine strawberries, arugula, basil, beets, peppers, tomatoes
Plant	chives, fruit trees and bushes, garlic, mint, onion and shallot sets, potatoes, rhubarb, tarragon	citrus trees
Harvest	chives, kale, leeks, microgreens, parsley, rhubarb, rosemary, sage, Swiss chard, thyme, windowsill herbs	

Late Spring

	Outdoors	Shade
Sow	American cress, arugula, beets, carrots, chicory, cilantro, corn, endive, Florence fennel, green beans, kale, kohlrabi, lettuce, mizuna, spinach, oregano, oriental mustard greens, parsley, peas, radicchio, radishes, runner beans, scallions, Swiss chard, thyme	basil, corn, cucumbers, eggplants, green beans, microgreens, runner beans, squashes, summer purslane, zucchini
Plant	Alpine strawberries, celery root, fennel, green beans, leeks, lettuce, mint, oregano, parsley, potatoes, rosemary, runner beans, thyme	citrus fruit, cucumbers, eggplants, peppers, tomatoes
Harvest	arugula, basil, beets, carrots, chives, chop suey greens, cilantro, fennel, gooseberries, kohlrabi, microgreens, mint, oregano, parsley, peas, radishes, rhubarb, rosemary, sage, scallions, spinach, strawberries, tarragon, thyme	

Early Summer

	Outdoors	Shade
Sow	American cress, arugula, beets, bokchoy, carrots, chicory, chop suey greens, cilantro, corn, corn salad, cucumbers, endive, green beans, kale, kohlrabi, lettuce, mizuna, oregano, oriental mustard greens, peas, radicchio, radishes, runner beans, scallions, spinach, squashes, tarragon, Witloof chicory, zucchini	basil, microgreens
Plant	celery root, corn, cucumbers, Florence fennel, kale, leeks, peppers, rosemary, squashes, tomatoes, zucchini	citrus fruit, cucumbers, eggplants, peppers, tomatoes
Harvest	American cress, arugula, basil, beets, carrots, cherries, chives, chop suey greens, corn salad, cucumbers, currants, fennel, gooseberries, herbs, kohlrabi, lettuce, microgreens, spinach, oregano, oriental mustard greens, peas, early potatoes, radicchio, radishes, rosemary, scallions, strawberries, Swiss chard, zucchini	

Outdoors　　　　　　　　**Shade**

Sow

American cress, arugula, beets, bokchoy, carrots, chop suey greens, cilantro, corn salad, kale, kohlrabi, mizuna, oriental mustard greens, radicchio, radishes, scallions, spinach, Swiss chard, tarragon, winter lettuce

microgreens

○ ○ ○ ○ ○ ○
save seeds!

Plant

kale, leeks, strawberries

Harvest

American cress, apples, apricots, arugula, basil, beets, blackberries, blueberries, bokchoy, carrots, cherries, chicory, chili peppers, chives, chop suey greens, cilantro, corn, corn salad, cucumbers, currants, eggplants, endive, fennel, figs, Florence fennel, garlic, green beans, lettuce, microgreens, mint, mizuna, nectarines, spinach, onions, oregano, parsley, peaches, pears, peas, peppers, potatoes, radicchio, rosemary, runner beans, sage, shallots, tarragon, thyme, tomatoes, squashes, strawberries, zucchini

---

Fall

Outdoors　　　　　　　　**Shade**

Sow

American cress, arugula, hardy peas, kohlrabi, radishes, winter lettuce

alpine strawberries, arugula, cut-and-come-again salad greens, microgreens

Plant

Garlic, strawberries, windowsill herbs, winter lettuce

Harvest

American cress, apples, apricots, arugula, beets, black- and blueberries, bokchoy, carrots, celery root, chicory, chives, chop suey greens, corn, corn salad, cucumbers, eggplants, endive, fennel, figs, green beans, herbs, kale, leeks, microgreens, mizuna, nectarines, onions, oriental mustard greens, peaches, pears, peppers, potatoes, radicchio, radishes, runner beans, strawberries, Swiss chard, tomatoes, winter squashes, zucchini

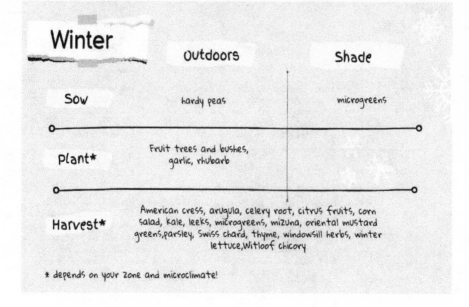

Winter

	Outdoors	Shade
Sow	hardy peas	microgreens
Plant*	Fruit trees and bushes, garlic, rhubarb	
Harvest*	American cress, arugula, celery root, citrus fruits, corn salad, kale, leeks, microgreens, mizuna, oriental mustard greens, parsley, Swiss chard, thyme, windowsill herbs, winter lettuce, Witloof chicory	

* depends on your zone and microclimate!

Now that we've dealt with the major components of setting up an urban garden, let's discuss strategies to keep your garden healthy and keep pests at bay. Chapter 8 is all about taking care of your garden and effective techniques to avoid mishaps.

CHAPTER 8

Managing Your Garden

Keeping Your Garden Healthy

As a plant grower, you need to be prepared for setbacks and unpleasant surprises. For instance, you may stroll into your garden one day and notice something odd in your plant's appearance: yellowing leaves, discolored patches, dark spots, or powdery white residue. In this chapter, we will go over the steps that you can take to avoid running into problems and keep your plants flourishing in every season.

Fit as a Fiddle

A plant catching a disease is the most mystifying thing. A jumble of questions may swirl inside your head: What could have caused it? How do you prevent it from spreading? How do you treat it? The disease triangle is the best way to understand disease prevention. Three factors must coincide to bring about disease in plants: a sick host (an unhealthy plant), a pathogen (fungus, bacteria, virus, or pest), and environmental conditions that favor the transfer of the pathogen to the host (high-humidity or drought).

Disease prevention involves knocking out one of the above factors. Here are some steps that you can take to protect your plants.

Keep an Eye Out for Problems

Inspect the leaves and stems for dead spots, rotting or insects before bringing new plants home. Observe the root quality. Place your hand on the soil with the stem between your fingers and turn the pot over. Shake it gently to loosen the roots from the pots. The roots should appear firm, white-colored and evenly spaced all over the rootball. Dark or mushy roots are a sign of trouble.

Use Fully Composted Waste

Make sure that the compost you use has fully decomposed. Proper composting makes the temperature soar, killing off any pathogens in the waste material. Leftover infected material can introduce potential disease in your plants if it hasn't degraded sufficiently.

Watch Out for Bugs

Insect damage usually gives viruses and bacteria access to plants. Pests such as aphids and thrips are responsible for the spread of impatiens necrotic spots. Leafhoppers transmit aster yellow disease to a range of host plants. Bug attacks put the plant under stress, making them susceptible to viral and bacterial diseases.

Clean Up Plant Debris

Pick up fallen dead leaves from the soil to prevent the spread of disease. Pathogens can overwinter on decaying leaves and plant debris, attacking new leaves in spring. For example, daylily leaf streak, iris leaf spot, and black spot on roses tend to spread from diseased leaves left to rot in containers. Similarly, blighted stems of tomatoes or potatoes should be burned or put in municipal waste rather than composted at home.

Choose the Correct Fertilizer

Too much of anything can be fatal, and the same holds true for fertilizer. An excess of fertilizer can burn the roots, disrupting water absorption. This makes the plants vulnerable to damage from extreme cold, heat, or drought. Plants deprived of essential nutrients tend to have stunted growth and are prone to disease.

The fertilizer you choose will ultimately depend on what you're growing and the nutrients you want to improve in the soil. You will notice three numbers mentioned on the fertilizer labels (for example, 5-10-15). The numbers correspond to the concentration of the macronutrients nitrogen (N), phosphorous (P), and potassium (K).

In addition to these, plants also require the following elements:

- **Calcium:** Improves the soil structure, necessary for plant cell membranes, neutralizes toxic materials and helps bind organic and inorganic particles.
- **Magnesium:** Necessary for photosynthesis because it makes up the only metallic component of chlorophyll.
- **Sulphur:** Crucial component of many proteins.

Lastly, plants require certain micronutrients to maintain health and vitality. These include boron, copper, zinc, iron, molybdenum, manganese, and chlorine. Since repeating watering can leach these nutrients from the soil over time, it's best to apply fertilizer to your plants regularly once every two to six weeks. While there are various options for fertilizers, an all-purpose fertilizer is usually the best place to start.

All-purpose fertilizers have all the macronutrients as well a few essential micronutrients such as manganese, zinc, and iron. Generally, to promote flower or fruit production, choose fertilizers with higher concentrations of phosphorous and potassium relative to nitrogen. Higher concentrations of nitrogen benefit foliar plants by encouraging more leaf growth. We will discuss plant fertilizers in more detail in the upcoming section and also learn a few simple recipes for making them at home.

Some additional tips to keep your garden in good shape include

- Prune the plants during late winter.

- Place the plants in your garden according to their preferred environmental conditions.
- Follow a consistent watering schedule.
- Avoid overcrowding plant containers in one spot, allowing plenty of airflow between them.

Crop Rotation

In Chapter 5, we learned the benefits of planting more perennials; however, most plants in our kitchen gardens are annuals. In addition to succession sowing (Chapter 1, *Planning to Maximize Your Space*) and companion planting (Chapter 5, *Companion Planting*), crop rotation is a necessity for annual crops.

Crop rotation involves growing different crops in succession in the same soil to replenish its lost nutrients. This practice helps prevent disease, limits the spread of pests, and creates healthy, well-balanced soil. The first step of crop rotation involves identifying the plant family of each crop. Here's a list of plant families to help you set up a five-year crop rotation plan for your raised beds and containers:

1. Solanums: Potatoes, peppers, eggplant, tomatoes
2. Brassicas: Cabbage, broccoli, kale, cauliflower, mustard
3. Legumes: Peas, green beans, kidney beans, lentils
4. Amaryllidaceae: Onions, garlic, leeks
5. Root vegetables: Beets, parsnips, carrots, celeriac, turnip, radish

All these plants have varying characteristics and nutritional requirements. Leafy plants such as kale and cabbage(brassicas) crave nutrients such as nitrogen, phosphorous, and potassium. Legumes' nitrogen-fixing ability makes them crucial for maintaining soil fertility. Potatoes and tomatoes tend to struggle with blight and other diseases; rotating these crops can help prevent these issues.

It's recommended to start by planting a nitrogen-fixing legume then move on to starving brassicas that'll appreciate the fertile soil. Solanums should be planted next, followed by industrious roots, which are adept at scavenging nutrients and minerals buried deep below the surface.

Fertilizer

A good quality fertilizer helps replenish lost minerals in the soil, so plants don't run out of essential nutrients. Generally, organic matter serves as a superb natural fertilizer; however, containers are usually devoid of soil life. Worm compost provides a rich source of plant nutrition; mixing a little worm compost with potting mix in the container before planting is a great way to set your plants up for success. Although applying the worm compost directly is generally the best option, sprinkling worm compost every now and then on top of the soil won't do the trick. It's better to mix everything by turning the soil with a small shovel. If you need to spread it over a larger area use liquid fertilizer instead.

Worm tea (the leftover liquid at the bottom of the wormery) serves as a fantastic liquid fertilizer, as does compost tea. (Chapter 3, *Feast for Your Plants*) The liquid at the bottom of a vermicomposting bin is called leachate, and it is not the same as compost tea (a common misconception). The leachate is not nearly as beneficial as compost tea, which involves putting the compost in a bucket of water (usually inside of a mesh bag to contain the solids), adding some sugar (like molasses, but not honey because it has antibacterial properties), and aerating it with a bubbler, or a small waterfall. This process gives the beneficial bacteria in the worm compost the oxygen and sugars they need to multiply.

Regardless of the kind of fertilizer you choose, it should be composed of the following elements:

1. Nitrogen (N): Stimulates stem and leaf growth
2. Phosphate (P): Strengthens root growth.
3. Potassium (K): Promotes flower and fruit production.

Different plant types require different fertilizers. For instance, leafy plants like spinach require plenty of nitrogen, as do tomatoes and peppers during the start of the season for developing strong stems and leaves. Later in the season, tomatoes need large quantities of potassium for fruit production. Commercially available all-purpose fertilizer contains a balanced concentration of each of the three major elements, making it an all-around satisfactory fertilizer.

Homemade Fertilizer

If you want to provide your plants the nutrition they require without splurging on store-bought fertilizer, here are seven homemade recipes you can try.

1. Epsom Salt Fertilizer

Epsom salt	1 tablespoon
Water	1 gallon (3.7 liter)

Mix and shake well. Apply the solution to your plants once a month during the growing season. Epsom salt provides plants with magnesium and sulfate, making it an excellent fertilizer for magnesium loving plants such as peppers, roses, tomatoes, and potatoes.

2. Used Coffee Grounds

Place a newspaper on a cookie sheet and spread your used coffee grounds, letting them dry completely for a few days. Mix the dried-up coffee grounds with the soil of your acid-loving plants that require nitrogen, magnesium, and potassium. They will slightly shift the soil pH toward acidic, which will benefit plants such as blueberries, rhododendrons, roses and azaleas.

3. Broken Eggshells

Save broken egg shells, letting them air dry and grinding them into a fine powder. Add this powder to your plant containers as a natural substitute for lime. The calcium carbonate present in the eggshells makes the soil pH slightly more alkaline, leading to better absorption of nitrogen, phosphorus, and potassium by the plants.

Mixing the eggshells with vinegar causes a reaction between acetic acid and calcium carbonate, making the calcium more bioavailable for the plants. Combining your broken eggshells and vinegar fertilizer techniques can be very powerful.

4. Vinegar Fertilizer

White vinegar	1 tablespoon
Water	4 cups

The acetic acid in the vinegar makes the soil pH more acidic, while killing weeds.

5. Fish Water

Simply pour old water from the fish tank into your containers instead of pouring it down the drain. Fish tank water is teeming with nitrogen and other nutrients necessary for plant growth.

Caring For Your Plants

As a gardener, you have to show your plants some TLC from time to time by giving them a little makeover. Deadheading, pruning, and pinching are crucial for potted plants to keep them looking healthy and preventing disease. Deadheading involves snipping dead blooms to encourage the plant to conserve its energy and produce more flowers.

Meanwhile, pruning is like giving your plant a haircut to keep it looking tidy and compact, and to promote new growth. Your plants may start looking a bit overgrown during the summer, which is a sign that you need to bring out your pruning shears and start chopping off some of those branches. Start by getting rid of weak, yellowing, or leggy growth and trim the rest of the plant to the desired size. Herbs such as basil and cilantro need regular pruning to forestall flowering, which can cause their leaves to taste bitter.

Lastly, pinching is a method of encouraging branching in young plants by breaking tender, young shoots with your fingers. You can make your plants bushier by removing the plant tip as the plant grows.

Key Takeaways

A gardener's work is never done. As you manage to grow sturdy plants from tiny seedlings, you must continue caring for your plants to fend off pathogens and keep them flourishing. But what happens if you walk into your garden one day and notice your favorite plant looking rather glum? If pests manage to elbow their way into your urban garden, don't despair—the next chapter is all about helping your plants recover from disease and restoring their strength. So, let's find out what it takes to nurse your plant back to health after catching disease.

What to Do When Things Go Wrong

Pests, weeds, and disease-causing organisms may be a nuisance for gardeners, but these life forms have an important place in nature. Simply put, these creatures are a part of nature's way to restore balance and keep plant populations in check. Without the check and balance system established by these pathogens and invasive insects, certain plant populations would outgrow others. As the dominant plant species use up all the nutrients in the soil, other plants begin to suffer, which leads to a sharp decline in in diversity and plant health.

Pests are a part of natural control systems that help maintain manageable levels of pests and hosts. Both play a crucial role by keeping each other's population in check. However, in an urban garden, disease or pests can spread rapidly, turning your months of labor to dust. You have to watch out for tiny critters and signs of microbial disease, so you can nip the problem in the bud. This might seem complicated if you don't know what to look for. Let's look at some common pests and the signs to watch out for.

What's Eating Your Plants? The Usual Suspects

Your urban garden is a big, free buffet for all sorts of bugs. You may not realize that these critters are busy chewing away your plants until you find brown spots on your fruits, white insects clustering around your tomato plants, and gaping holes in the leaves.

Common plant bugs include leaf- and flower-eating caterpillars, beetles, mites, leaf miners, and bark borers. Let's look at the signs of different pests, so you can get rid of them before they cause significant damage to your garden.

Leaf Miners

- They are the larvae of flies, sawflies, and moths.
- They create long white trails on the leaves.
- They mostly attack vegetables such as lettuce, squash, beans and peas.
- Their spread can be controlled through companion planting. Lambsquarter and columbine can be used to distract them.

Cutworms

- They are plump little caterpillars that curl up in the soil during the day and come up to the surface to feed only at night.
- They feed on leaves, stems, roots, and seedlings.
- They can cause the plant to topple over, shrivel, and die.
- You can place aluminum or cardboard collars around transplants to create a barrier. These will stop cutworm larvae from feeding your plants.

Grubs

- They are the larvae of beetles that live under the soil, feeding on the roots and stems of plants.
- They can cause stunted plant growth.
- They can be detected by taking the plant out of the soil and observing the roots, which will show visible signs of damage.
- They cause more damage by attracting other animals such as rodents, raccoons, and skunks, if left untreated.
- There are plenty of methods available to control their population depending on the grubs type. One of them is Neem oil.

Wireworms

- They are the larvae of click beetles.
- They have cylindrical, wirelike yellow or brown bodies.
- They chomp down seeds, roots, and tubers like potatoes.
- They cause poor growth, yellowing, and wilting.
- Steinernema carpocapsae (SC) nematodes – also nicknamed as NemAttack – are the most effective control for wireworms.

Leafcutter Ants

- They attack fresh vegetation like young stems, leaves, and flowers.
- They suck the plant sap, causing the plant to become weak.
- Neem-oil mixture works well against them, and you also can try covering their trails with cedar mulch.

Borers

- They are the larvae of beetles, moths, and wasps.
- They burrow into the stems of raspberries, roses, and blackberries.
- They leave the stems hollow, causing stunted growth and wilting leaves.
- They also affect cucumbers, squash, melons, and pumpkins.
- The best trick to control them is to cover your plants and limit pest access to the cultivation area.
- You can also set up pheromone traps to catch adult borers.

Cabbage Loopers

- They are smooth, green caterpillars with thin white lines that run vertically across their body.
- Their backs arch into a loop when they crawl, earning them their unique name.
- Their larvae feast on a range of plants such as lettuce, cabbage, carnations, nasturtiums, tomatoes, beets, potatoes, parsley, and spinach.
- They create small, irregular holes on the leaves.

- Bacillus thuringiensis is very effective against cabbage loopers.

Aphids

- They are tiny, pear-shaped creatures, ranging in color from green to black.
- They feed on tender stems, sucking plant sap and depriving the plant of essential nutrients.
- They produce honeydew, which is a white, sticky, sugary substance that attracts ants and fungi. Ants actively 'farm' aphids, which causes them to bunch together near stem tips and makes them much easier to spot.
- The fungi and ants may carry the mosaic virus to the plant, causing yellow, disfigured leaves and flower buds.
- Planting marigolds will help control them in your garden.

Spider Mites

- These are tiny mites that live under leaves, feeding on plant sap and giving the leaves a mottled yellow appearance.
- They make fine silvery webs that are sometimes visible on the underside of the leaves.
- They can be controlled by raising humidity levels or using organic sprays, like dish soap-water mixture.

Gall Mites

- These microscopic mites feed on plant sap, causing abnormal growth.
- They cause raised red bumps on the leaves that resemble pimples.
- They can also lead to the appearance of clumps of matted hairs on the leaves.
- Gall Mites are mostly harmless and don't cause serious damage.
- They can be controlled by using liquid lime sulfur or simply cutting the affected area.

Thrips

- Thrips create white blotches on the leaves and cause brown leaf tips.
- They are tiny, winged insects, almost invisible to the naked eye.
- They mostly attack vegetables such as cucumbers, peas, tomatoes, and onions.
- Neem Oil is known as one of the best sprays for garden thrips control.

Whiteflies

- They are tiny white moths that stick to the underside of leaves.
- They feed on the sap of plants, depriving them of essential nutrients.
- They cause yellowing and dropping of the leaves.
- They may fly out in a big white cloud, if you grab the stem and give it a shake.
- You can attract whitefly-eating predators by planting fennel, calendula, oregano, parsley, buckwheat and thistles. You also can make a vinegar mixture (based on the recipe in the next chapter) to get rid of them.

Organic Methods of Pest Control

Organic pest control aims to control pest populations without damaging the environment. Artificial pesticides tend to leave their residue on fruits and vegetables, which may cause harm to the person consuming them. Moreover, they kill a wide range of insects, which may be beneficial for our plants. Excessive use of chemical pesticides can also drive away pollinators from your vegetable and fruit garden, causing a significant reduction in harvest.

The word "organic" refers to substances that are naturally found in the environment and contain carbon. Organic methods of pest control include a range of natural products that successfully get rid of harmful insects and pathogens, such as pyrethrum, lime, sulfur, soaps, vinegar, and salts.

You can keep your garden healthy by putting up barriers to keep the pests out and encouraging beneficial insect populations that feed on them. Strong, healthy plants are capable of defending themselves. So, providing your plants with the necessary nutrition and watering regularly goes a long way in protecting your garden.

In addition to taking better care of your plants, you can nip problems in the bud by keeping an eye out for signs of disease. Some changes in your plants that could signal trouble include leaf curling, dropping, and yellowing and the appearance of sticky honeydew on the foliage. Stunted plant growth and decreased fruiting and flowering are also signs that your plant needs help. Keep in mind that these can also be the signs of under- or overwatering, as well as of various nutrient deficiencies. A combination of symptoms is usually required for an accurate diagnosis.

You can prevent attacks by planting flowers alongside your crops to bring beneficial insects such as lacewings and ladybugs to your urban garden. These tiny little helpers feed on pests, keeping your garden disease free. Another reason to opt for organic methods is that pesticides may harm beneficial insects, leading to more problems down the road.

Most pest problems can be avoided by using barriers such as fleece and netting to protect your plants or using sticky sheets to catch moths before they lay their larvae. However, I'm not a big fan of this method, since it can also catch beneficial insects.

Buying pest-resistant cultivars and using fresh compost can also contribute toward reducing pest problems. Copper tape placed around cloches and pots can help deter snails and slugs. The copper reacts with the slime produced by these creatures, producing mild electric shocks that stop them in their tracks. Another ingenious method to ward off pests and weeds is companion planting (Refer to Chapter 5, *Companion Planting)*. For example, planting onions near carrots can help keep carrot flies at bay. Herbs such as parsley, dill, and cilantro also help attract beneficial insects while driving out harmful pests.

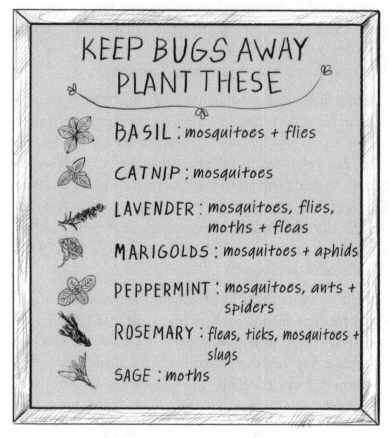

Figure 8.1: Herbs can help you keep the bugs away.

Tiny insects and invisible microorganisms are not the only invaders to watch out for: hungry birds and rodents can also cause significant damage to your crops. Netting is an effective solution for keeping out large predators. You can support it with canes and weigh it down at the base so that it doesn't get blown away by strong winds.

In addition to the above, here are some effective strategies for getting rid of garden bugs and preventing disease:

- *Handpicking*: Pick insects that are visible to the eye like cutworms, and beetles, cabbage loopers and drop them into soapy water to kill them.

- *Diatomaceous Earth (DE)*: Sprinkle DE around your plants. It can penetrate the exoskeleton of several pests such as leafhoppers, cutworms, and root maggots, causing dehydration and killing them off.

- *Bacillus thuringiensis (Bt)*: Spray *Bt* solution around your plants to get rid of harmful pests. When this organic insecticide is consumed by pests, it produces proteins that paralyze their digestive system, causing them to stop feeding and die. It does not harm beneficial insects such as earthworms, nematodes, and ladybugs.

- *Water:* Hose down the plants with a blast of water to knock off pests like aphids, spider mites, and whiteflies.

- *Soap and water mixture*: Mix one teaspoon of dish soap or soap dissolved in one quart of water and spray on the plant to get rid of spider mites, aphids, thrips, and whiteflies. You can also add vegetable oil to this mixture. The oil coats the bodies of the aforementioned insects, suffocating them.

- *Neem oil*: Mix two teaspoons of neem oil and one teaspoon liquid soap dissolved in one quart of water and spray on your plants to eliminate aphids, leafhoppers, whiteflies, and scale insects.

- *Vinegar mixture:* you can easily create your own insecticidal soap from a gallon (3-7 liter) water, 2 tbs white vinegar, 2 tbs dish detergent, and 2 tbs baking soda. Spray this mixture under the leaves of the plants where white fly eggs, scale and adults reside.

- *Discard affected plant parts*: Cut and dispose of affected plant parts to limit spread of disease.

Deep in the Weeds

Weeds tend to be less prolific and easily controlled in containers because, unlike garden soil, homemade and commercially produced compost is mostly free of weed seeds. However, weed seeds can get blown into the soil in your containers, so keep a look out for tiny seedlings, plucking them out as soon as possible.

Big, perennial weeds like dandelions and weeds with long tap roots can be lifted from the soil with a hand fork. These pernicious weeds can be difficult to remove, especially when their roots become entwined with the roots of your plant. It's important to remove these wild plants before they begin flowering and produce more seeds. A thick layer of mulch prevents sunlight from reaching the seeds of wild plants, limiting their spread (*Check Chapter 3, How to Keep Soil Healthy*).

Key Takeaways

Unsightly holes in leaves, herbs nibbled to the ground, and plants that simply won't grow can be frustrating to witness in your garden. However, resorting to inorganic insecticides or pesticides has major disadvantages. Organic methods of pest control offer effective and inexpensive solutions to put an end to your gardening woes.

Getting rid of unwelcome guests in your urban garden can be as easy as picking them off the plants or simply spraying a homemade pesticide solution. You can prevent a number of insects and microorganisms from marching into your garden by setting up barriers. Keeping your plants healthy by watering them regularly and keeping the soil well balanced with nutrients are simple tricks to avoid running into problems.

In the next section, we will discuss harvesting your produce. We will explore preserving and storing techniques, so the fruits of your labor don't go to waste. With all the hard work behind us, it's time to reap the harvest!

CHAPTER 9

It's Time to Harvest

A huge amount of time, effort, and perseverance goes into growing a plant and bringing it to the stage of producing fruits. Harvesting produce is the end goal of every fruit and vegetable gardener. The prospect of our hard work materializing into delicious fresh food is what keeps us going.

Harvest season is bound to get you feeling excited, but it's also an opportunity for you to maximize your gains with some useful tips and tricks. Let's look at some harvesting techniques and preservation methods to do justice to your urban garden's bounty.

Principles for Harvesting Vegetables

While you can rely on seed packets and plant tags for lots of useful information about a plant, the number of days before maturity is generally not a good indicator of when vegetable and fruit will ripen, due to temperature fluctuations. A chilly spring can cause them to ripen later than usual, while heatwaves during the summer can make your produce ripen sooner. Other factors that affect ripening include soil fertility, and low or high precipitation. All this can make predicting the day of maturity challenging for gardeners.

Fortunately, your plants are always dropping clues about their state of maturity. Keeping a close eye on your fruits and vegetables can help you pick up the subtle changes signaling ripeness. Here are some factors to keep in mind as you get your basket ready for plucking those big red tomatoes, peaches, eggplants, and other vegetables and fruits:

- *Flavor and nutrition:* Harvest fruits and vegetables at the peak of their nutrition and flavor. Vegetables such as beans, peas, turnips, and summer squashes reach their best flavor and are packed with the most nutrition when they are tender and immature. On the other hand, tomatoes, winter squash, and melons must ripen completely on the vine to completely develop their flavor.

- *Size and color:* Pick fruits and vegetables when they are the right size and color, as it is a good indicator of maturity. Check seed packets to find out the size and color of mature vegetables and fruits.

- *Frequency of harvest*: Pick ripe vegetables and fruits from the plant as often as possible. Not harvesting regularly can cause them to over ripen and decrease the quantity of subsequent produce. For example, unpicked beans become tough and lose their nutritional value. Meanwhile, a two-inch-long (5 cm) zucchini can transform into a 2-foot-long (60 cm) club in a few days.

- *Harvesting tools*: Use the right tools for harvesting your crops. For example, lettuce, peas, and kale can be pinched or snapped off with your hands, but you may require scissors to cut off vegetables such as beans. Plants with tough stems like eggplants and cucumbers may require a sharp knife or pruners.

- *Handling plants:* Train plant vines over trellises or add support to your containers to avoid stems bending or breaking. Don't pull or rip vegetables or fruits from the plant, as it can cause tears, providing an easy access point for disease.

- *Sequence of harvest:* Start with the large, outer leaves of leafy vegetables such as lettuce, leaving the inner, newer growth.

Here are some tips for different crops to help you decide the right time and tips for picking different crops:

Beans (Snap)

- Pick when the pods reach their fullsize, before the seeds inside start bulging.
- Harvest often.

Beans (Lima)

- Harvest when the pods and seeds reach their full-size, but before the pods turn yellow.
- Feel the end of the pod; it should feel spongy.
- Shell a few pods to check; the pods and seeds should taste fresh and juicy.

Beets

- Pull the beets when they are 1 to 2½ inches (2.5 – 4 cm) in diameter; larger ones are not as flavorful and can become woody.
- Dig up the roots before the first hard freeze.

Broccoli

- Harvest when the head is 3 to 6 inches (7.5 – 15 cm) in diameter and dark green with compact buds.
- Cut them 6 to 7 inches (15 – 18 cm) below the flower heads.
- Harvest before the buds turn yellow or bloom into flowers.
- Leave the plant in the ground after the main head is harvested, as subsequent, smaller spears often regrow.

Brussel Sprouts

- Harvest when the sprouts are between 1 and 1½ inches (2.5 – 4 cm) in diameter.

- Break the sprouts by twisting at the base of the plant when they feel firm.
- Pinch out the growing tip of the plant to get more sprouts.
- Pick after one or two light frosts for maximum flavor.

Cabbage

- Harvest when the head reaches the size of a softball and feels firm to the touch.
- Avoid delaying picking the vegetables, because they will continue to grow and split open due to excessive water uptake.

Bok Choy

- Pick when the plant reaches its full-size: 12 inches (30 cm) for large varieties and 6 to 8 inches (15 -20 cm) for dwarf types.
- Use a knife to cut the plant at the base an inch above the soil.
- Alternatively, harvest progressively by cutting the outer leaves first.

Carrots

- Harvest when the carrots are an inch in diameter.
- Check the size of the carrots by pulling one up by the leaves.
- Collect spring-planted carrots as soon as they mature, else they may become bitter and fibrous due to the summer heat.

Cauliflower

- Harvest when the head is regular-shaped, before it splits or turns yellow.
- Cut the stem below the head with a sharp knife.
- Avoid waiting too long to harvest, because the cauliflower heads may start splitting.

Chard

- Pick when the leaves are about 6 inches (15 cm) long.
- Snip the outer leaves, leaving the heart of the plant to produce more leaves.

Cucumbers

- Harvest 50 to 70 days after planting.
- Avoid leaving the cucumbers on the vine for too long because they can develop a bitter taste over time.
- Pick the fruit usually eight to ten days after the first flowers bloom.
- Make sure to pick the cucumbers before they start showing signs of yellowing.
- Pick the fruits that feel firm and have dark green flesh.
- Look for cucumbers that are 6 inches (5-15 cm) long.
- Remove the fruits that seem stunted or show rotten ends to prevent the plant from wasting its energy on them.
- Use pruners or garden shears to avoid damaging the vine by twisting and pulling.
- Cut the stems ¼ inch (6 mm) above the cucumber and handle them with care to avoid bruising.

Lettuce

- Harvest when it is full-size but young and tender.
- Pick young leaves because mature leaves taste bitter and woody and can spoil quickly.
- Remove the outer leaves, leaving the inner young leaves.
- Harvest butter head, romaine and loose-leaf types by snaping off the outer leaves, digging up the entire plant or snipping the plant an inch above the soil surface.
- Harvest crisphead lettuce by picking when the center is firm.

Peppers

- Harvest sweet varieties 60 to 90 days after planting while the very hot types may take up to 150 days.
- Add 8 to 10 weeks to the harvest time mentioned on the seed packet if you are growing from seeds to make up for the time between sowing and transplanting.
- Harvest hot varieties of peppers such as jalapenos when the fruit turns dark green.

- Pick other varieties such as Serrano, Anaheim, Tabasco, Cayenne, or Celestial when the color shifts from green to orange, reddish brown, or bright red.
- Harvest frequently to encourage the plant to produce more fruits.
- Use pruners, scissors, or a sharp knife to cut the peppers from the plant.

Tomatoes

- Harvest tomatoes at the end of the growing season in late summer.
- Pick the tomatoes when they are bright red in color (unless you choose a variety of tomato that ripens in another color like brown, purple, yellow, orange, green, or white).
- Check the ripeness of the fruit by picking one tomato and placing it in a bucket of water. Ripe tomatoes will sink to the bottom.
- Gently squeeze the fruit to check its firmness.
- Hold the fruit and pull gently while holding the stem with your other hand.

Peas

- Harvest 60 to 70 days after planting; however, this may vary for some varieties.
- Use one hand to hold the pea vine while gently pulling the pea pods with the others.
- Store in a cool area after picking such as a cold water bath and dry later.
- Eat them fresh or store in the refrigerator for up to a week.
- Blanch and place in zip lock bags before putting them in the freezer for a year-long supply.

Radishes

- Avoid leaving spring radishes in the ground past their age of maturity because they will become tough and taste starchy.

- Leave winter radishes in the ground for a few weeks after they mature, harvesting them just before frost.
- Check the seed packet to estimate time of harvest since different radishes have different lengths of growing periods.
- Pull one out as a test to check if they are ready.
- Harvest when the green growth above the soil reaches 6 to 8 inches.
- Look or feel for the top part of the radish pushing out of the top soil.

Potatoes

- Harvest on dry days by digging gently so as to not puncture the tubers.
- Dig up the potatoes when the first hard frost is expected to avoid frost damage to the tubers.
- Harvest new potatoes that are small in size and have tender skins 2 – 3 weeks after they stop flowering.
- Harvest mature potatoes 2 – 3 weeks after the foliage turns brown and dies.
- Cut the foliage before digging up the tubers.
- Prepare the potatoes for harvest and storage by watering occasionally after mid-August.
- Wait 10 to 14 days more after cutting the foliage to allow the potatoes to develop thick skins. However, avoid waiting too long because they may begin to rot due to the moisture in the soil.
- Dig a small hole to observe the potato skins if you are unsure whether it is the right time for harvest.

Strawberries

- Pick shiny, red berries by gently pinching off the stem.
- Make sure to handle them with care, as they can get damaged easily, causing premature rotting.
- Pick off overripe strawberries so they don't attract pests.
- Rinse, dry, and place in the refrigerator.
- Wash and store in the freezer for later use.

Citrus Fruits

- Harvest ripened fruits that are heavy and appear vibrant in color.
- Use garden shears or clippers to snip the stem above the fruit.
- Refrigerate your harvest to keep them viable and fresh.
- Freeze the zest for later use.
- Freeze fruit juice in ice cube trays for cooking later.
- Dehydrated citrus fruits can be used in teas and broths.

Apple

- Harvest fruits that are firm and have smooth skins with vibrant color. Avoid picking apples prematurely because they may taste sour.
- Avoid delaying harvesting as it may lead to soft, mushy, over ripened fruits.
- Hold the apple and twist to detach the fruit from its stem.
- Store in the refrigerator to keep them viable and fresh for a long time.
- Can or freeze excess apples or turn them into sauces and apple pie filling. You also can make apple cider or vinegar. Dehydrated apple slices are one of the best snacks, especially with a bit of cinnamon.

Calendula

- Pick or snip off the flower where it meets the stem.
- Avoid picking flower heads that are dry and going to seed.
- The calendula leaves and petals are both edible. The leaves are a bit bitter but go well mixed into a salad. Choose fresh blooms or petals as a garnish, seasoning, tea, or yellow colorant, and use the older ones for seed saving.

Lavender

- Harvest by cutting the stems just before the flowers bloom.
- Tie the stems and hang the flowers in a sheltered place to dry.
- Shake the dry flowers from the stems and store in a container.

Seed harvesting makes it extremely economical to plant your next batch of crops, so you don't have to go through the trouble of buying transplants or seed packets. Here are two methods of harvesting seeds and preparing them for storage:

Dry Fruited Harvesting:

Plants like lettuce, grains, beans, peas, sweet corn, carrots, sweet peas, spinach, onion, beets, and many herbs produce seeds that dry while being attached to the plant. Just leave these plants in the garden after their prime, allowing them to "go to seed," and you can harvest the seeds once they've dried.

Wet Fruited Harvesting:

Plants like tomatoes, squash, and berries have membranes around the seeds, so they don't germinate inside the plant. You must remove this membrane to save the seeds for future sowing. You can do this by removing the seeds, placing them in a sieve or fine colander, and rubbing the pulp away under running water.

Seed Storage

You can store seeds simply by placing them inside a paper envelope and labeling the seed variety and the date of its harvest on the outside. Keep the envelope in a glass jar with an airtight lid and store in a cool, dry place where the temperature remains stable. High humidity, moisture, and temperature fluctuations can be detrimental for seeds. If stored correctly, most seeds remain viable for two to three years.

Here are some tips for saving seeds of different plants:

Beans:

- Harvest the seeds when the pods dry, turn brown, and begin to open.
- Dry the pods for two weeks by placing them on waxed paper before shelling.
- Store the seeds in an airtight container.

Cucumber:

- Harvest the seeds when the plant ripens and the fruit dries.
- Cut the cucumbers in half and remove the pulp with the seeds.
- Place them in a container of water and let them ferment for two to four days at room temperature.
- Make sure to stir the mixture occasionally.
- Collect the good seeds that will sink to the bottom of the container by pouring out the remaining mixture on top.
- Rinse the seeds with water.
- Place on waxed paper and let the seeds dry for a week.
- Store in an airtight container.

Peas:

- Collect the seeds when the pods start drying, turn brown, and start splitting open.
- Let the pods dry for two weeks before shelling.
- Store in an airtight container.

Pepper

- Harvest the seeds when the fruit ripens.
- Wait for the peppers to turn red and begin to shrivel.
- Remove the seeds and dry them on waxed paper for two to four days.
- Keep in an airtight container.

Tomatoes

- Collect the seeds when the fruit ripens.
- Squeeze out the pulp and the seeds in a container filled with water.
- Allow the pulp to ferment for a few days at room temperature, making sure to stir occasionally.
- Collect the good seeds that will sink to the bottom and pour out the pulp.
- Rinse the seeds and place on waxed paper.
- Let them dry for a week and place in an airtight container.

Onions

- Start harvesting onion seeds when the flower heads begin turning brown.
- Carefully cut the stalks a few inches below the head and put them in a paper bag.
- Place the bag in a cool, dry place and wait for a weeks.
- Shake the heads when they dry to release the seeds.

Carrots

- Let the seed heads fully ripen on the plant.
- Cut the flower heads when they begin to brown and become dry.
- Place the flower heads in a small, paper bag and let them dry.
- Place in sealed plastic or glass containers once the seed heads have completely dried and shake vigorously to collect the seeds.
- Keep the seeds in an airtight jar and store in a cool dry place.

Dills

- Wait for the seeds to turn from green to brown.
- Harvest the seeds when the umbels turn inward and the seeds are in clumps.
- Use scissors or garden shears to cut the stalk a few inches from the base of the flower.
- Place the seeds in a paper bag and let them dry.
- Store in a dry area for a week or two.
- Shake to release the seeds and store in an airtight container in a dark cupboard, like other spices.

Lettuce

- Harvest the seeds once they form clusters topped with white fluff like a dandelion flower.
- Allow the seeds to dry while on the plant and either collect them individually every day or place a paper bag on the seed heads, tying it at the base, so none of the seeds are lost.

Asian Greens

- Allow the seed pods to dry on the plant.
- Cut the brown seed heads when they feel brittle.
- Pound the seed pods with a pestle or in your palms to release the seeds.
- Place in a container and shake gently to separate heavier seeds from the chaff, which you can later pick with your fingers.
- Finish the winnowing process by blowing into the container so the light pieces of pod float away, leaving behind heavy seeds.

Radishes

- Harvest when they start seeding in early to mid summer.
- Wait for the seed pods to turn brown, leaving them attached to the plant as they dry.
- Place a paper bag over the seed heads and tie at the base to avoid the seeds scattering in the wind.

Saving Seeds from Bolted Vegetables

Bolting or "running to seed" is when a vegetable starts flowering out of the blue, causing plant growth to stop. While bees and butterflies may love the blooms, this is a great opportunity for you to collect seeds. For example, lettuce usually bolts in hot weather. Bolting in lettuce is usually indicated by swelling in the middle of the stalk of the flower head.

The leaves turn tough and bitter tasting. Instead of harvesting them for food, you can use them for collecting seeds. Wait until lots of seed pods appear then shake them and collect the seeds. Store them in a cool, dry place.

Why Should You Save Seeds?

Saving seeds is an excellent idea for several different reasons. For starters, it is a great way to help you save money. Generally, a packet of 50 pepper seeds can cost up to $3 or more. Meanwhile, transplants can cost $5 each. So harvesting seeds from the plants you have already grown is more economical option that allows you to be self-sufficient.

By saving seeds, you can also increase the population of plants with traits that you desire. So if you harvest a tomato that tastes absolutely divine, saving the seeds of that particular tomato plant means you can enjoy the flavorsome fruit time and again. Waiting for the flowers to produce seeds can also give rise to insect pollinators, bringing more bees, butterflies and beetles to your container garden and increasing genetic diversity.

Plant Types for Seed Saving

Plants produce seeds in various ways. Knowing your plant and its seed-producing method can help you harvest the seeds at the right time and store them properly.

Self-Pollinating Plants

These plants don't require pollen transfer from one flower to the other, and do not rely on external carriers. Their successive generations don't show drastic changes in their characteristics, so their features tend to remain constant. Tomatoes, beans, peas, and peppers are some examples of self-pollinating plants. Seeds of these plants don't require special treatment before storage. Seeds from biennial plants like beets and carrots are usually more difficult to harvest, since gardeners must wait for two growing seasons before setting the seeds.

Cross-Pollinated Plants

Plants like corn and most vines have separate male and female flowers that cross-pollinate, i.e., the pollen is transferred from the flower of one plant to the other. The seeds of these plants may exhibit varying characters. For example, corn can pollinate sweetcorn growing in a nearby garden on a windy day, affecting the flavor of the offspring. Insects can also cross-pollinate melons, squash, pumpkins, gourds, and cucumbers, leading to strange new varieties. It's important to keep this in mind while saving the seeds of these plants and watching out for variants in the next growing season.

Open-Pollinated Plants

We discussed open-pollinated seeds (for more details check out also the *Seed Vocabulary* at the end of the book). Many open-pollinated varieties are heirlooms, passed down through generations by gardeners. These are plants that can self-pollinate as well as cross-pollinate with other plants of the same variety. Their seeds produce plants that are very similar to the parent plant. For example, tomato varieties such as "The Big Rainbow," "San Marzano," and "Brandywine" are open pollenated. The seeds of these plants produce offspring that are nearly identical to the parent plants, so make sure to choose the most vigorous plant with the most flavorful fruits for seed saving.

Hybrid Plants

Hybrid plants are created when two different varieties combine due to cross pollination. The combination sometimes produces desirable traits, creating high-yielding plants with remarkable vigor and disease resistance. Tomatoes such as "Big Boy," "Beefmaster," and "Early Girl" are some examples of hybrid plants. However, since the plants produced from the seeds of these plants are not completely identical to the parent plants, it is impossible to predict how the seedling plant will perform or the characteristics of the fruits.

Key Takeaways

Following the gardening practices outlined in this book will guarantee an abundant harvest. The process of picking fruits and vegetables may seem simple, but as we learned in this chapter, there's a lot more to it than yanking them from the plant. Methods of harvesting produce vary depending on the plant type. Moreover, fruits and vegetables are not the only useful plant parts that can be harvested. Seed saving is an ingenious technique that helps cut costs of buying seed packets and transplants.

While the methods of preservation listed in this chapter provide effective solutions for dealing with excessive produce, the recipes in the next chapter will be a delight for your taste buds.

CHAPTER 10

From the garden to your table

If you end up with a generous harvest, then storing and preserving your produce will allow you to enjoy the rewards of your labor all year long. There are various methods of preserving fruits and vegetables. Let's discuss a few of the most popular techniques.

Preservation Techniques

Freezing

The easiest way to preserve your food is simply sticking it in the freezer. Almost all vegetables are suitable for this method except for cabbage and potatoes, which may become limp and waterlogged. You may need to blanch most vegetables first, which involves boiling them for one to three minutes. Blanching stops enzymatic activity, preserving flavor, color, and nutrition. Dip the vegetables in cold water after blanching to cool them quickly before packing in plastic containers or freezer bags and stowing them in the freezer.

Canning

Canning is the most well-known method of preservation, but it has to be done properly or some foods may spoil due to bacterial contamination. Most fruits and some vegetables respond well to a boiling water bath; however, low-acid vegetables like peas, beans, carrots, corn, and squash may need a pressure canner to do the trick.

Dehydration

Dried fruits and vegetables can be easily rehydrated for using in soups or casseroles. You can either buy an electric food dehydrator or dry the produce in the oven or in bright sunlight. Vegetables such as peppers can be hung on a string in a cool, well-ventilated room and allowed to dry.

Pickling

You can pickle a wide range of vegetables such as carrots, cabbage, beets, asparagus, beans, peppers, and tomatoes. Firm vegetables such carrots and beets may require blanching to make them tender. Pickling can be achieved by placing the vegetables in a glass jar and adding seasonings such as turmeric, cumin, mustard seeds, dill, celery seeds, jalapeno peppers. A brine solution containing vinegar, pepper, and salt is prepared by boiling these ingredients and is poured over the vegetables once it cools. Finally, the jar has to be sealed securely to avoid contamination.

Fermenting

One of the oldest food preservation techniques, fermenting can help you put your excess harvest to good use. Countless veggies and fruits can easily be fermented. For example, you can turn cabbage into delicious sauerkraut by adding salt and water. Fermented cucumbers taste similar to homemade dill pickles, while fermented carrots are crunchy and delicious.

Fermenting recipes are fairly simple and straightforward, involving a few key ingredients like vinegar, sugar, salt, and a variety of add-ins like lime juice, lemon, celery seeds, herbs, mustard seeds, and spices.

My simplest yet bulletproof recipe is using a plain 2% salt liquor (1 liter water + 20 g salt) on top of the vegetables.

Storage

Some vegetables can be easily stored in a cool, clean place for up to a year. Vegetables ideal for storage include potatoes, squash, and onions. A container filled with moist sand is best for storing root crops like carrots and beets. You can also leave root crops in the ground during winter by covering them with a 12-to-18-inch (30-45 cm) layer of mulch.

Storage conditions vary for different vegetables. Temperature and humidity are the most important factors. Three combinations that are perfect for long-term storage are

- Dry and cool: 50 - 60°F (10 - 15°C), 60 % relative humidity

- Dry and cold: 32 - 40°F (0 - 4°C), 65% relative humidity

- Moist and cold: 32 - 40°F (0 - 4°C), 95% relative humidity

The shelf-lives of your vegetables get shortened up to 25% for every increase of 10°F (-12°C). Since some of the above conditions are difficult to create in our homes, here are some places that are perfect for food storage:

Basements

Basements are usually cool and dry, making them perfect for vegetable storage. However, make sure to provide some form of ventilation to prevent fungi such as molds from spoiling your food.

Refrigerators

These are excellent for vegetables that prefer dry and cold conditions such as garlic and onions. Placing them in perforated plastic bags can help generate cold, moist conditions, but only for a limited amount of time. Unperforated plastic bags may create too much humidity, leading to condensation, which may promote growth of bacteria or mold.

Cellars

Cellars are the perfect spot for foods that prefer moist and cold conditions. However, as with basements, make sure to provide good ventilation and create barriers for keeping the food safe from rodents. Materials such as straw, hay, or wood shavings can also be used as insulation to protect your food from rapid temperature fluctuations.

Preserve Through Cooking

By the time harvest season comes to a close, my refrigerator is not only chock full of frozen preserves, but also delicious sauces, chutneys, and pickles. Turning excess fruits and vegetables into pastes and sauces is an excellent way to maximize the space in your refrigerator. Whenever you're craving out-of-season foods, all you need to do is pull out a jar and dip your spoon in and taste the heavenly flavor. So, let's put on our chef's hats and get cooking!

Pesto

You can toss your pasta in it or spread it on baked potatoes, pizzas, and bread. Regardless of how you choose to eat it, the combination of fresh basil and garlic is a treat for your taste buds. And the best part? It only takes 15 minutes to make.

Ingredients

Fresh basil leaves	2 cups
Freshly grated Romano or parmesan cheese	½ cup
Olive oil	½ cup
Minced garlic (1 tablespoon)	3 cloves
Chopped pine nuts or walnuts	⅓ cup
Salt	¼ teaspoon
Black pepper	⅛ teaspoon

Method

In a food processor, begin by pulsing the basil and pine nuts. Add the cheese and garlic and pulse again. Make sure to scrape the sides of the food processor with the rubber spatula. Gradually pour the olive oil into a thin, steady stream as the processor is running to help it emulsify and prevent the oil from separating. Add salt and sprinkle freshly ground pepper before tossing it with pasta for a quick sauce. Dollop it over baked potatoes or spread it over crackers or toast.

Green Tomato Pickle

I planted eight plants in my backyard this year that were soon weighed down by the tomatoes. A few weeks ago, I had to prune some low-hanging branches and ended up with almost six pounds of green, unripe tomatoes. I wasn't sure how to use them all, so I turned to Google and found a green tomato pickle recipe. It came out so good that I decided to make it again in the future.

Ingredients

Green tomatoes	1 - 2 lbs (0.5-1 kg)
Green chilies	6 - 7 green chilies
Chopped ginger	1 tablespoon
Mustard seeds	1 teaspoon
Turmeric powder	½ teaspoon
Fenugreek seeds	½ teaspoon
Chili powder	3 tablespoons
Curry leaves	10 leaves
Lemon juice	⅛ cup
Oil	⅛ cup
Salt	⅛ cup

Method

Wash the tomatoes and cut them in half. Heat oil in a small wok or pan and add the mustard and fenugreek seeds. Turn the flame off and add chili powder and turmeric while mixing it with a spoon. Let the mixture cool down before grinding it to a powder. Heat the remaining oil in a pan and add ginger, curry leaves, green chilies, and salt. Add tomatoes and cover the lid, letting it cook for half an hour. Add lemon juice and cook for another ten minutes. Turn the flame off and take off the heat. Pour the mixture in a clean glass jar once it cools and add the remaining oil on top. Refrigerate and enjoy with plain rice or alongside other foods to give an extra kick of flavor.

Tomato Sauce

A staple for every kitchen, a generous spread of tomato sauce is essential for pizza and pasta. Use tomatoes harvested in August and September, when they tend to be the ripest, to make a large batch of tomato sauce. Choose sweet, blood red tomatoes with thick flesh. You can pour the prepared tomato sauce in zip-lock bags and freeze or fill glass jars and keep in the fridge.

Ingredients

Tomatoes	5 lbs (2.3 kg)
Salt	¾ teaspoon
Olive oil	2 tablespoons
Tomato paste	1 tablespoon
Garlic	1 clove
Basil	1 sprig
Bay leaf	1 leaf

Method

Wash the tomatoes and cut them in half. Squeeze the seeds out and set some aside for storage (Refer to Chapter 9). Grate the tomatoes and discard the flesh. You should have 4 cups of grated tomato pulp. Place it in a wide saucepan over high heat. Add salt, oil, tomato paste, basil, garlic, and bay leaf. Bring it to a boil then lower the heat and let it simmer.

Reduce the sauce until only half of it remains. Stir occasionally to prevent it from burning or sticking to the bottom of the pan. You should get about 2½ cups of sauce after ten to fifteen minutes. It will stay good in the fridge for five days and longer if frozen.

Radish Relish

This rosy colored relish is perfect for your spring radishes. It goes well with pretty much everything: hot dogs, barbeque chicken, hamburgers, you name it!

Ingredients

Cubed radishes	3 cups
Celery	2 large
Red onion	1 large
Salt	2 teaspoons
Sugar	1 cup
Mustard seeds	1 tablespoon
Vinegar	1 cup

Method

Grind the radishes, celery, and onion or chop them finely. Mix the rest of the ingredients and leave the mixture for three hours. Boil in a large pan and cook for ten minutes. Pour into jars, leaving a half inch space at the top. Close the lids and give a 20-minute water bath in ½ pint (1/4 liter) boiling water if you want to can them.

Fire cider is an herbal tonic considered to increase immunity, help with digestion, and warm you up on a cold winter day. The basic recipe combines horseradish, ginger, garlic, onions, turmeric and hot pepper dissolved in apple cider vinegar. The hot peppers make it fiery, the honey and the spices create a unique immune boost. The concoction sits in a mason jar for about 30 days to infuse.

Figure 5.1: Homemade fire cider recipe.

The bountiful harvest from your urban garden can turn into a delicious spread. The recipes above provide creative ways for you to store herbs and vegetables, so they don't take up too much space.

Now that we've reached the end of our urban gardening journey, let's round up all the things we've learned so far and shed light on the road ahead.

Conclusion

As our urban gardening journey winds to a close, I hope the methods outlined in this book helped you gain greater insight into the fascinating world of container gardening, and develop confidence to create your green space in an urban setting. The aim of this book was to challenge the restrictions we tend to place upon ourselves and provide city dwellers the tools and ideas to indulge in the pleasure of gardening.

We started our journey by questioning the limitations of our living spaces and working out creative, out-of-the-box solutions for finding the best microclimates for our plants and utilizing our gardening space to the fullest. We learned the subtle differences in containers based on their shape, size, and material and how to match them with our plant's requirements.

We developed keen insight into the soil required for growing our plants and learned different methods of enhancing its quality such as homemade composting, mulching, and worm farming. Topics such as watering, sowing, planting, managing, and harvesting plants may seem deceptively simple, but, as we learned in this book, can be a little complicated. However, the information compiled in this book will help you navigate these murky waters with ease!

When I started learning about urban gardening, I realized it had the potential to transform our homes and our lives for the better. It opens the door for living a zero-waste, sustainable, and self-sufficient life. The principles outlined in *Successful Container Gardening* will have your homes overflowing with plants, your pantry stocked, and your dinner table laden with scrumptious food, all while having a minimal impact on the environment.

It's time to turn your hobby into something productive. Let nature into your home and enjoy the perks of gardening.

Sophie

Thanks for Reading,
Please Leave a Review!

I would be *incredibly appreciative* if you could rate my book or leave a review on **Amazon**.

Just scan this QR code with your phone, or visit the https://hardcover-SCG.sophiemckay.com link to land directly on the book's Amazon review page.

Your review not only helps me create better books, but also helps more fellow gardener experience success in the garden and put healthy food on their family's table.

Thank you!

What to Read Next?

If You Liked This Book, Try This One Too!

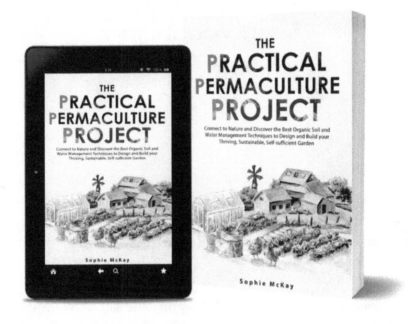

Unlock the secrets of a resilient garden! Discover permaculture design and **learn how to grow your own food in harmony with nature**.

Join Sophie on a guided tour and create your own **sustainable permaculture garden** with confidence. Success guaranteed!

Just scan this QR code with your phone, or visit the https://book.SophieMckay.com link to land directly on the book's Amazon page.

Seed Vocabulary

First-time gardeners may find selecting seeds and the complicated jargon that comes with it rather daunting. To help novice growers through this complex process, here's a list of all the difficult terms you'll most likely encounter as you go seed shopping (Barth, 2016):

Cool Season Crops

Frost-tolerant plants that flourish in spring and fall when the daytime temperature hovers between 60 and 70°F (15 and 21°C) and nighttime temperatures swing between 30 and 40°F (-1 and 4°C).

Warm Season Crops

Plants that thrive in late spring and early fall, preferring 80°F (26°C) in the day and 50°F (10°C) during the night.

Days to Maturity

The average number of days it takes for a plant to mature after sowing the seeds in the ground or transplanting seeds grown indoors to the garden.

Disease Resistant

Includes acronyms such as VFN and VFNTS, which reference the disease that seeds are resistant to. For example, VFN tomato seeds can survive verticillium wilt, fusarium wilt, and nematodes.

Heirloom

These are traditional plant varieties passed down through generations that are different from the seeds produced by modern seed breeders because these seeds are carefully selected for their flavor, productivity, hardiness, and adaptability. Most heirlooms were created before the 1940s.

Open Pollinated (OP)

Those plants that can be pollinated naturally by insects or wind. Professional breeders use controlled pollination techniques, producing seeds that require special methods for pollination. OP plant seeds can be stored each year, as they will give rise to "true" plants that are identical to the parent plant.

F1 Hybrid

These include seeds created by crossing two different plants. F1 hybrid seeds give rise to plants with superior traits; however, these seeds can't be saved and planted the next year again, as their offspring will be different from the parent plant.

Non-GMO

Seeds that are not created using genetic engineering techniques.

Pelleted Seed

Seeds coated with a biodegradable substance to make them larger and easier to plant. This reduces overplanting of tiny seeds such as those of lettuce and carrots.

Bibliography

Albert, S. (n.d.). *Hardy, Half-hardy, and Tender Vegetable Crops*. Harvest to Table.

Andrychowicz, A. (n.d.). *Winter Sowing Seeds: A Quick-Start Guide*. Get Busy Gardening.

Barth, B. (2016, January 21). *How to Shop for Veggies: Our Seed-Selection Guide*. Modern Farmer.

Bauer, E. (n.d.). *Fresh Basil Pesto Recipe*. Simply Recipes.

Bordessa, K. (2021, July 16). *Container Vegetable Gardening for Beginners*. Attainable Sustainable.

Can You Start Composting in Urban Areas? (2019, June 24). Greenhouse Emporium.

Chadwick, P. (2020, October 5). *Guidelines for Harvesting Vegetables*. Piedmont Master Gardeners.

Chase, A. (n.d.). *10 Ways to Keep Your Garden Healthy - FineGardening*. Fine Gardening. Retrieved September 12, 2022.

Container Gardening Secrets: Ideas to Inspiration. (n.d.). Eartheasy Guides & Articles. Retrieved July 26, 2022.

Container garden maintenance tips: Help your plants thrive all summer long. (n.d.). Savvy Gardening.

164

Daron. (2020, March 24). *Nitrogen Fixers – What They Are and Tips to Get Started*. Growing with Nature.

Dyer, M. H. (2022, January 10). *How To Preserve Vegetables From Garden: Learn Methods Of Preserving Vegetables*. Gardening Know How.

The Earth Box. (n.d.). *How to Grow a Self-Sufficient Garden*.

18 Best Plants for North Facing Balcony Garden. (n.d.). Balcony Garden Web.

Ellis, B. (2016, March 1). *How to Give Your Seeds a Head Start Before Planting*. Refresh Living.

Engels, J. (2016, November 18). *How and Why to Rotate Your Annual Crops - The Permaculture Research Institute*. Permaculture Research Institute.

Fischer, N. (2018, January 4). *The 14 Best Seed Companies to Plant in Your Organic Garden*. Nature's Path.

Green Tomato Pickle. (n.d.). Aayis Recipes.

Harvesting Guide. (n.d.). Kellogg Garden Products.

Hassani, N. (2021, November 29). *Companion Planting with Companion Planting Chart*. The Spruce.

How do we choose which Seed Varieties to Plant? (n.d.). Broadfork Farm.

How to Speed up Seed Germination. (n.d.). Frostproof Growers Supply.

Huffstetler, E. (2022, July 5). *How to Make Your Own Fertilizer*. The Spruce.

Hughes, M. (2022, August 27). *How to Save Seeds from Your Garden to Plant Next Year*. Better Homes & Gardens.

Judd, A. S. (n.d.). *The Best Way to Water Outdoor Potted Plants*. Growing In The Garden.

Judd, A. S. (n.d.). *Best Way to Water Raised-Bed Gardens*. Growing In The Garden.

Kanuckel, A. (2022, June 20). *Companion Planting Guide: Sow Easy*. Farmers' Almanac.

Kellogg Garden Organics. (n.d.). *Creating a Pollinator Friendly Garden*.

Kemp, J. (2013). *Permaculture in Pots: How to Grow Food in Small Urban Spaces*. Permanent Publications.

Kime, L. (2012, August 28). *Soil Quality Information - Articles Articles*. Penn State Extension.

Know Your Growing Zone: Cold Hardiness and Heat Tolerance. (2013, November 15). Longfield Gardens.

Lopez, C. (n.d.). *Different Types of Soil for Gardening*. Trinjal.com.

MacArthur, A. (n.d.). *How to Mix Your Own Potting Soil for Container Vegetables*. Food Gardening Network.

MacKenzie, J., & Grabowski, M. (n.d.). *Saving vegetable seeds | UMN Extension*. University of Minnesota Extension.

Magyar, C. (2020, January 14). *Annuals, Biennials and Perennials - 3 Plant Types You Need To Know*. Rural Sprout.

Markham, D. (n.d.). *8 Natural & Homemade Insecticides: Save Your Garden Without Killing the Earth*. Treehugger.

Masabni, J. (n.d.). *Mulching - Should you water before or after mulching?* Texas A&M AgriLife Extension.

Mayntz, M. (2021, March 15). *Different Types of Hummingbird Feeders*. The Spruce.

McKay, S. (2022). *The Practical Permaculture Project*.

Michaels, K. (2022). *Vegetable Container Gardening for Beginners*. The Spruce.

Michaels, K. (2022, June 15). *Six Great Containers for Growing Vegetables*. The Spruce.

Peischel, W. (2022, September 16). *Rats to the rescue: could pesky rodents finally get New Yorkers composting?* The Guardian.

Painter, T. (2018, December 14). *What Kind of Soil Do You Use in Containers for Vegetables?* Home Guides.

Patterson, S. (n.d.). *Which Soil Is Best for Plant Growth? | LoveToKnow*. Garden.

Rievley, S. (2020, February 3). *How to Install a Rain Barrel System*. HGTV.

Rosy Radish Relish Recipe. (n.d.). Food.com.

SanSone, A. (2021, March 25). *15 Best Plants That Attract Pollinators - Best Flowers for Pollinators*. The Pioneer Woman.

Selection of Seeds- Factors To Consider While Selecting Seeds. (2016, May 7). Ugaoo.

Tanis, D. (n.d.). *Quick Fresh Tomato Sauce Recipe - NYT Cooking*. NYT Cooking.

Thompson, R. (2018, June 18). Gardening for health: a regular dose of gardening. *Clinical Medicine, 18*(3), 201 - 205. 10.7861/clinmedicine.18-3-201

Tong, C. (n.d.). *Harvesting and storing home garden vegetables | UMN Extension*. University of Minnesota Extension.

Vinje, E. (2012, December 7). *How to Make Your Own Potting Soil*. Planet Natural.

Whittingham, J. (2012). *Fruit and Vegetables in Pots*. DK Pub.

Witte, D. (2020, August 17). *How to Build Nutrient-Rich Soil on the Permaculture Garden: New Life On A Homestead*. New Life On A Homestead. Retrieved July 25, 2022, from https://www.newlifeonahomestead.com/nutrient-rich-soil-permaculture/

Zafar, S. (2020, June 5). *What is Vermicomposting*. EcoMENA. Retrieved August 2, 2022, from https://www.ecomena.org/vermicomposting/

Printed in the USA
CPSIA information can be obtained
at www.ICGtesting.com
LVHW090325231123
764661LV00003B/296